D0823788

J 823.914 MAL v.01
Maltese, Racheline
The book of Harry Potter
trifles, trivias &
particularities
WITHDRAWN 101308

ROCKFORD PUBLIC LIBRARY
Rockford, Illinois
www.rockfordpubliclibrary.org
815-965-9511

THE BOOK OF

TRIFLES, TRIVIAS & PARTICULARITIES

VOLUME ONE

Conjured by

RACHELINE MALTESE

PUBLISHERS

STERLING & ROSS PUBLISHERS

NEW YORK § TORONTO

ROCKFORD PUBLIC LIBRARY

THE BOOK OF HARRY POTTER TRIFLES, TRIVIAS & PARTICULARI-
TIES ©2007 Racheline Maltese. Copyright under the Berne Copyright Con-
vention, Universal Copyright Convention and the Pan-American Copyright
Convention.

No part of this book may be used or reproduced, stored in a retrieval system or
transmitted in any form, or by any means, electronic, mechanical, photocopied,
recorded or otherwise, without written permission of the publisher except in
the case of brief quotations embodied in critical articles and reviews.

Disclaimer: This book is not endorsed, approved, or authorized by Warner
Bros., J. K. Rowling, or her publishers. Harry Potter is a trademark of Warner
Bros. Entertainment Inc.

Published by Sterling & Ross Publishers
New York, NY 10001
www.SterlingAndRoss.com

Cover design by Nicola Lengua.
Composition and typography by Rachel Trusheim.

Library of Congress Cataloging-in-Publication Data

Maltese, Racheline, 1972-
   The book of Harry Potter trifles, trivias & particularities / by Racheline Maltese.
      p. cm.
   Includes bibliographical references.
   ISBN-13: 978-0-9779545-2-0 (alk. paper)
   ISBN-10: 0-9779545-2-8 (alk. paper)
   1. Rowling, J. K.--Characters--Miscellanea--Juvenile literature. 2. Potter, Harry (Fictitious character)--Miscellanea--Juvenile literature. 3. Hogwarts School
of Witchcraft and Wizardry (Imaginary place)--Miscellanea--Juvenile literature.
4. Children's stories, English--Miscellanea--Juvenile literature. 5. Fantasy fiction, English--Miscellanea--Juvenile literature. 6. Literary recreations--Juvenile
literature. I. Title.
   PR6068.O93Z7634 2007
   823'.914--dc22

                              2007037265

                  Printed in the United States of America.

CONTENTS

INTRODUCTION

KEY

⋆ QUEST 1 ⋆

Hogwarts & Academia • 11 •

⋆ QUEST 2 ⋆

Potions & Spells • 45 •

⋆ QUEST 3 ⋆

The Magical Menagerie • 75 •

⋆ QUEST 4 ⋆

Everyday Magic • 111 •

⋆ QUEST 5 ⋆

Government, Banking & Bureaucracy • 141 •

✶ QUEST 6 ✶
Sports, Entertainment & Leisure • 171 •

✶ QUEST 7 ✶
Famous Families & Faces • 203 •

✶ QUEST 8 ✶
History & Legend • 237 •

✶ QUEST 9 ✶
The Wizarding Wars • 267 •

www.harrytrivia.com

INTRODUCTION

Welcome to *The Book of Harry Potter Trifles, Trivias and Particularities*! You are about to embark on nine Quests that will test your knowledge and cleverness when it comes to the world of "The Boy Who Lived."

You will be tested in the following categories: Hogwarts & Academia; Potions & Spells; The Magical Menagerie; Everyday Magic; Government, Banking & Bureaucracy; Sports, Entertainment & Leisure; Famous Families & Faces; History & Legend; and The Wizarding Wars.

In each Quest you will be presented with 75 questions in three different skill levels labeled Salamander, Phoenix and Dragon. The Salamander, being the smallest and most harmless of these fire Beasts, represents the easiest questions. The Dragon, being the largest and most dangerous of these creatures, represents the most difficult. The Phoenix, an exceedingly rare and often benevolent creature, can surprise you with its power, and so similarly the questions at this skill level should not be underestimated.

Some questions will have short, specific answers drawn from a given chapter of a given book, but others will require you to combine facts you've learned in different places in the course of the series and then puzzle out the habits of the wizarding world based on them. If you get stuck along your journey, you will find hints suggesting other ways to approach tricky questions and pointers about where in the series to find your solution.

Answers, which include the book and chapter citations for where they were found or an explanation of how they were arrived at, are located at the end of each 75-question set. If you are keeping score, you should correctly answer 20 out of 25 questions at any given skill level in order to consider yourself a master of that skill level in the Quest. Throughout the answer section you will also find additional trivia facts about the books as well as the intersection of Muggle and wizarding history, culture, mythology and habit.

The questions have been drawn from the seven-book series (HP1-HP7) chronicling Harry's adventures as well as the two wizarding books J. K. Rowling penned to benefit Comic Relief U.K.: *Fantastic Beasts and Where to Find Them* (FB) and *Quidditch Through the Ages* (Q). While trivia on some of the differences between the Harry Potter books and the Harry Potter films is provided throughout, none of the questions require that you've seen the films about Harry's epic struggle with Voldemort.

To paraphrase the immortal words of Albus Dumbledore, if you are ready, if you are prepared, you may begin!

QUEST KEY

Skill Level One

 The Salamander

Skill Level Two

 The Phoenix

Skill Level Three

 The Dragon

QUEST 1
HOGWARTS & ACADEMIA

Hogwarts School for Witchcraft and Wizardry lies at the heart of the wizarding world. Most of its British students are educated there, and many of its best minds teach there. Thanks to Albus Dumbledore and Harry Potter it became a critical focus in each of the two wars with Voldemort. The very nature of its founding highlights the social questions that form the basis for centuries of strife within the magical world. Without Hogwarts, the wizarding world as we know it would not exist.

On this first Quest your knowledge of all things Hogwarts will be tested. It's time to remember those wondrous classes, challenging textbooks, difficult professors, strange traditions, odd occurrences, intense house rivalries, and, of course, the very magic of the castle itself.

Remember, the Salamander questions are simple, the Phoenix questions are puzzling, and the Dragon questions are just plain difficult. Ready? Begin!

THE QUESTIONS

1. Name each Hogwarts house, colors and associated animal.

2. What candy is associated with Albus Dumbledore?

3. What type of cauldron is a required school supply for all Hogwarts students?

4. Name each of the wizarding schools that competed in the Triwizard Tournament during Harry's fourth year.

5. What type of brooms did Lucius Malfoy buy for the Slytherin Quidditch Team in Harry's second year?

6. Who won the House Cup in each of Harry's school years?

HINTS!

Hagrid stopped Harry from buying a set of solid gold cauldrons in *Harry Potter and the Sorcerer's Stone*, ruling out one type of material. To get this question right, you'll need to know both the material the cauldron is made of and its size.

7. Name the founders of Hogwarts.

8. Ron and Harry took the Patil twins to the Yule Ball. Who took whom?

9. How do you open the Chamber of Secrets?

10. How does one open *The Monster Book of Monsters*, a required text for Care of Magical Creatures, without being bitten?

11. Who are the abandoned boys of Hogwarts?

12. Name all the ghosts of Hogwarts.

HiNTS!

Remember that only certain people with a very special skill can open the Chamber. So aside from knowing where the opening to the Chamber is, you must remember one of the unique traits Harry and Voldemort have in common.

13. What are O.W.L.s and N.E.W.T.s and what do they stand for?

14. What do the House-elves call the Room of Requirement?

15. Name three passwords to Dumebledore's office.

16. Of which school team was Eileen Prince the captain?

17. Name all the classes offered at Hogwarts.

18. Name all of Gilderoy Lockhart's books.

HINTS!

Luckily, Dumbledore liked to change the password to his office a lot, meaning that you don't have to remember all his passwords to get the question right. If you need to guess, try candies.

19. Which band played at the Yule Ball in Harry's fourth year?

20. On what date did the other schools competing in the Triwizard Tournament during Harry's fourth year arrive?

21. What organization gives the O.W.L.s and N.E.W.T.s?

22. Who was headmaster of Hogwarts before Albus Dumbledore?

23. When was Hogwarts founded?

24. Who wrote *Unfogging the Future?*

HINTS!

Wizarding examinations are overseen by the Ministry of Magic. The group, abbreviated W. E. A., doesn't seem to be designated as part of any particular department though. What does W. E. A. stand for?

25. In which tower is the Divination classroom located?

26. How do you get into the Room of Requirement?

27. Name three passwords to the Gryffindor common room.

28. Which tower is Hogwarts' tallest?

29. What is the password for the Slytherin common room?

30. What is the motto of Hogwarts and what does it mean?

HINTS!

Like Dumbledore's office, these passwords change all the time. Usually, they are created by the Fat Lady, but sometimes Sir Cadogan helps out, which should give you plenty of ideas of where to look in the books for these.

31. In which tower is the Owlery located?

32. Of what type of wood are the main doors of Hogwarts made?

33. What awards did Tom Riddle win at Hogwarts?

34. What guards the staffroom?

35. Name the gemstones in the house points hourglasses.

36. Hogwarts has how many staircases?

HINTS!

Tom Riddle won two awards at Hogwarts, neither for dishonesty, although at least one award, related to the Chamber of Secrets, was obtained that way.

37. How many House-elves live and work at Hogwarts?

38. In what way did Neville Longbottom redecorate the Defense Against the Dark Arts classroom?

39. What interaction with a painting is necessary to get to Hogwarts' kitchens?

40. Where does the Sorting Hat live when not in use?

41. How many secret passages lead in and out of Hogwarts?

42. Where is the caved-in passage out of Hogwarts located?

Hints!

Remember that the animation and sentience of wizarding paintings doesn't just apply to those with human subjects. In fact, animals, vegetables or even fruits might want to talk with you. There's no word on minerals at this time.

43. The Shrieking Shack is said to be what?

44. What types of trees are in the Forbidden Forest?

45. To what tune is the Hogwarts school song sung?

46. How does Binns enter and exit his classroom?

47. How does one make the Whomping Willow stop whomping?

48. What does the statue of the humpbacked witch hide?

HINTS!

Much to the chagrin of many, in some ways it is impossible to get this Hogwarts school song question wrong.

49. What time does the library close?

50. Why does Moaning Myrtle's bathroom not function properly?

51. What caused Salazar Slytherin to split with the other founders?

52. What town do students who are third years or older (and have parent or guardian permission) get to visit on occasion?

53. How do you gain access to the library's Restricted Section?

54. Who was the caretaker at Hogwarts before Argus Filch?

HiNTS!

By using an Invisibility Cloak and breaking in, is not actually a valid answer. However, the Trio's forays into the Restricted Section will help you understand just how restricted it really is. Or isn't.

55. Miranda Goshawk is the author of which series of Hogwarts texts?

56. Name the species that live in the Hogwarts lake.

57. What documentation receives the most dedicated space in Filch's office?

58. How many sets of work robes are first year students required to bring to Hogwarts?

59. Where did Fred and George Weasley find the Marauder's Map?

60. In accordance with which Educational Decree is Dolores Umbridge made Head of Hogwarts?

HINTS!

While it's probably just good laundry policy it's worth considering which number is generally a charm.

61. The father of which of Harry's peers was on the Hogwarts Board of Governors during the first half of their school careers?

62. Who is the author of *Defensive Magical Theory*?

63. What power does Educational Decree Number Twenty-three give to Dolores Umbridge in her role as Hogwarts High Inquisitor?

64. What mode of transportation does not work within Hogwarts?

65. Who told Ron that being sorted hurts?

66. To what did Hagrid attribute Professor Quirrel's stutter?

HINTS!

While it sounds like something a certain Slytherin might say, it's actually just one of Ron's brothers. Which?

67. How many textbooks were required for first years when Harry started at Hogwarts?

68. What type of familiars are permitted to students?

69. Who wrote *The Dark Forces: A Guide To Self-Protection*?

70. By when must a student reply indicating that he or she will or will not attend Hogwarts?

71. Who is the author of *Magical Theory* (not to be confused, hopefully, with the aforementioned *Defensive Magical Theory*)?

72. What color should the fastenings on a student's cloak be?

HiNTS!

Despite the animals we see various students in possession of, there are actually only three basic types of familiars allowed. Ron is breaking the rules with his.

73. Where in Diagon Alley do students purchase their uniform robes?

74. What is the difference between how first years get to Hogwarts and how returning students arrive?

75. How many titles were listed for Albus Dumbledore on the letter extending Harry admission to the school?

THE ANSWERS!

1. Gryffindor, red and gold, a lion; Hufflepuff, yellow and black, a badger; Ravenclaw, blue and bronze, an eagle; Slytherin, green and silver, a snake.

TRIVIA TIDBIT

BOOK VERSUS MOVIE

While the house colors for Ravenclaw are blue and bronze in the books, in the films, they are blue and gray or silver. This was reflected in the Hogwarts and house crests as well as the student uniforms.

2. The sherbet lemon or lemon drop is the candy Dumbledore most frequently offered his visitors.

TRIVIA TIDBIT

BRITISH VERSUS AMERICAN

The lemon drop familiar to American readers of *Harry Potter and the Chamber of Secrets* is a sherbet lemon for British readers. Sherbet is most commonly a type of frozen treat to Americans and presumably this is why the name of the candy was changed to avoid confusion. Changes to J. K. Rowling's text have been made on several occasions to accommodate differences in British and American English, the most notable one being the name of the first book in the series. It appeared in England as *Harry Potter and the Philosopher's Stone* and in the United States as *Harry Potter and the Sorcerer's Stone*. This difference in naming was retained in the films, with all English-language releases outside of the United States (including Canada) being *Harry Potter and the Philosopher's Stone*.

 3. A pewter cauldron in size 2 (HP1, chapter 5).

4. Hogwarts School of Witchcraft and Wizardry, Beauxbatons Academy of Magic, and Durmstrang Institute (HP4, chapter 12).

TRIVIA TIDBIT

BOOK VERSUS MOVIE

The film version of *Harry Potter and the Goblet of Fire* portrayed Beauxbatons and Durmstrang as each being single-sex schools. However, in the book, they were both coeducational.

5. Nimbus 2001 (HP2, chapter 4).

6. Gryffindor won the House Cup in each of Harry's first three years. In his fourth year, the winner of the cup was not specified at the closing feast, possibly due to Cedric Diggory's death during the Triwizard Tournament at the hands of Voldemort. In Harry's fifth and sixth years, we also do not know the winner of the House Cup, although it was presumably awarded; Harry merely had larger concerns. In what would be his seventh year we could assume that the House Cup competition continued due to a reference during the Battle of Hogwarts in HP7 to the gem-filled hourglasses that are used to track house points. However, due to the war it was unclear whether the House Cup was ultimately awarded that year.

7. Godric Gryffindor, Helga Hufflepuff, Rowena Raven-claw and Salazar Slytherin.

8. Harry's date was Parvati, and Padma accompanied Ron. However, it seemed clear that Harry would have rather been with Cho Chang and Ron with Hermione or at least hiding in the Gryffindor dormitory so that no one could see his dress robes (HP4, chapter 23).

9. The Chamber of Secrets must be told to "open up" by someone speaking Parseltongue in front of its en-trance, which is located behind a sink, labeled with a small snake, in one of the bathrooms on the second floor. The Parseltongue command reveals a large pipe that leads to an underground passage and then to the Chamber itself (HP2, chapter 16). Up until *Deathly Hallows*, only Tom Riddle, Harry Potter, and presumably the Chamber's cre-ator, Salazar Slytherin, are known to have opened the cham-ber. However, Ron, having memorized the Parseltongue phrase, succeeds in opening the chamber during the Battle of Hogwarts in order to collect Basilisk fangs for he and Hermione to use as weapons.

10. While extreme agility might help one avoid wounds thanks to the ferocious nature of *The Monster Book of Monsters*, the simplest way to open it safely is to pet it (HP3, chapter 6). It seems not even Flourish and Blotts

knew this since they were storing the books in cages when Harry went to purchase his (HP3, chapter 4).

11. Voldemort (as Tom Riddle), Severus Snape and Harry Potter. It was Harry Potter who came up with this moniker for himself and the two wizards with whom he had half-blood status, powerful magic, and a difficult childhood as common bonds despite the fact that Voldemort was always his mortal enemy and that Snape was an ongoing source of confusion, frustration and rage (HP7, chapter 34).

12. The Hogwarts ghosts for whom we have names are: Nearly Headless Nick (properly Sir Nicholas de Mimsy Porpington), The Bloody Baron, The Fat Friar, Moaning Myrtle, The Grey Lady and Professor Binns. However, there are at least fifteen other Hogwarts ghosts for which we do not have names since the castle is said to contain more than twenty ghosts (HP1, chapter 7). If you answered this question correctly, you also successfully recalled that Peeves, a poltergeist, is not a ghost at all.

13. O.W.L.s and N.E.W.T.s are wizarding standardized tests. They stand for Ordinary Wizarding Levels and Nastily Exhausting Wizard Tests, which are taken at the end of fifth year and seventh year respectively. O.W.L.s and N.E.W.T.s are offered in all class subjects (except Flying)

that are taught at Hogwarts and different numbers of these tests and levels of achievement on them are recommended or even required for different careers.

Trivia Tidbit

Wizards & Muggles

While standardized testing is familiar to students from all over the world, J. K. Rowling designed the O.W.L.s and N.E.W.T.s to be the wizarding equivalent of the tests taken by British students. These tests include the Ordinary Level or O-Level, which has been phased out in favor of the General Certificate of Secondary Education (GCSE), and the Advanced Level (or A-Level), although a number of other qualifications exist. These and similar tests are also commonly used in former British colonies and the Commonwealth nations, but there has not yet been any word on the adoption of O.W.L.s and N.E.W.T.s outside of wizarding Britain.

 14. The Come and Go Room (HP5, chapter 28).

15. In chronological order, the following passwords were used to gain admittance to Dumbledore's office: lemon

drop or sherbet lemon (HP2, chapter 11 – nomenclature depends on country where the book was released), cockroach cluster (HP4, chapter 29), fizzing whizbee (HP5, chapter 22), acid pops (HP6, chapters 9 and 10).

16. Gobstones (HP6, chapter 25).

17. Throughout the series we learn that Ancient Runes, Arithmancy, Astronomy, Care of Magical Creatures, Charms, Defense Against the Dark Arts, Divination, Flying, Herbology, History of Magic, Muggle Studies, Potions and Transfiguration are all offered at Hogwarts, but not all are required subjects of study.

18. Gilderoy Lockhart is credited as the author of a number of texts: *Break with a Banshee, Gadding with Ghouls, Holidays with Hags, Magical Me, Travels with Trolls, Voyages with Vampires, Wanderings with Werewolves,* and *Year with the Yeti* each of which were required school texts in Harry's second year (HP2, chapter 4). He is also the author of *Gilderoy Lockhart's Guide to Household Pests* (HP2, chapter 3) and possibly other books unknown to us. Since we now know that Lockhart used Memory Charms to *Obliviate* those who actually took the adventures written about in his books, there is speculation of a ghost writer, who, of course, may or may not have been a ghost, but by now has most surely been *Obliviated.*

TRIVIA TIDBIT

BOOK VERSUS MOVIE

According to J. K. Rowling's books, Gilderoy Lockhart had only written nine books for which we have names. However, a tenth book, *Who Am I?*, appears at the end of the film version of *Chamber of Secrets*, demonstrating that while Lockhart may no longer know who he is, thanks to a Memory Charm that backfired, he's certainly still vain.

 19. The Weird Sisters (HP4, chapter 23).

TRIVIA TIDBIT

BOOK VERSUS MOVIE

In the film *Harry Potter and the Goblet of Fire* an orchestra conducted by Professor Flitwick played the formal music that the champions, their dates and others waltzed to at the opening of the ball. Only later did The Weird Sisters play the wizarding world's version of rock music. In the book, however, they played a slow tune for the initial dance and there was no indication of Professor Flitwick's involvement with any of the event's musical choices.

20. October 30th (HP4, chapter 15).

21. The Wizarding Examinations Authority (HP5, chapter 31).

22. We do not actually know who was headmaster of Hogwarts directly before Albus Dumbledore. Armando Dippet was the headmaster when Tom Riddle was a student at the school and the Chamber of Secrets was opened, but the historical chain of command at Hogwarts is not well documented for the reader, nor is it entirely clear in what year Dumbledore became headmaster, although it was surely before the arrival of the Marauders based on a variety of statements including those of Snape, Lupin and Dumbledore himself.

23. Hogwarts was over one thousand years old at the time of the books, but an exact date of its founding was not given or, in fact, known (HP2, chapter 9; HP4, chapter 12).

24. *Unfogging the Future* is by Cassandra Vablatsky and was the assigned textbook in Divination when Harry took it. (HP3, chapter 4).

25. The North Tower (HP3, chapter 6).

26. You must walk past the empty wall behind which it is located three times while concentrating on that which is needed. If someone is using the room, it is impossible to enter it without knowing the purpose to which it is currently being put or coincidentally desiring the room for the same purpose. Otherwise it seems (but there is no manual to confirm this) that the room gives precedence to whoever is using it at any given moment. We learned of the properties of the Room of Requirement over time as Harry and others used it in books five and six (HP5, chapter 18 provides the most details).

27. Chronologically, the known passwords for the Gryffindor common room are: caput draconis (HP1, chapter 7), pig snout (HP1, chapter 9), wattlebird (HP2, chapter 5), fortuna major (HP3, chapter 5), scurvy cur (HP3, chapter 11), oddsbodikins (HP3, chapter 12), flibberti-gibbet (HP3, chapter 15), balderdash (HP4, chapter 12), fairy lights (HP4, chapter 22), banana fritters (HP4, chapter 25), Mimbulus mimbletonia (HP5, chapter 11), dillig-rout (HP6, chapter 12), baubles (HP5, chapter 15), absti-nence (HP6, chapter 17), toffee eclairs (HP6, chapter 20), tape worm (HP6, chapter 23), quid agis (HP6, chapter 24). The constantly changing passwords for the Gryffindor common room may speak to high security or a constant need to change passwords due to leaks; which opinion you hold surely depends on your own house affiliation.

28. The Astronomy Tower (HP1, chapter 15).

29. "Pure-blood" is the only password we were ever told of for the Slytherin common room (HP2, chapter 12). This seems excessively simple for a house known for cunning when compared to the frequently changing and harder to guess Gryffindor passwords, but perhaps Slytherin House was merely close-knit enough that no other passwords were ever leaked to outsiders.

30. Hogwarts' motto was often seen by many for the first time in the front matter of the books: "Draco dormiens nunquam titillandus." Meaning in Latin, "Never tickle a sleeping Dragon." Unlike much of the Latin-like verbiage in the series, this is actually a correct and valid phrase in the classical language.

31. The West Tower (HP4, chapter 15).

32. The doors are made of oak, but are either enchanted in some fashion or are otherwise magical since Flitwick was able to instruct them to recognize Sirius Black (HP3, chapter 14).

33. Tom Riddle received an award for special services from the school for accusing Hagrid of being the one who

opened the Chamber of Secrets (HP2, chapter 13). This led to Hagrid's expulsion from Hogwarts and the breaking of his wand, and allowed Riddle to maintain his own innocence. Riddle also won a Medal of Magical Merit, but what earned him this award is not currently known.

34. Two gargoyles that have no qualms about giving an attitude with students who attempt to get into the room (HP5, chapter 17).

TRIVIA TIDBIT

MAGIC, MYTH & MUGGLES

As an architectural term, gargoyle refers to a grotesque statue on a building that is used to funnel water away from its roof or sides. While gargoyles popularly refer to all figures with such appearances, chimera is the term reserved for such statues that don't have this water-related function. In literature the gargoyle is often portrayed as some sort of animate stone creature, often evil, that can detach itself from its building at will; they are often winged.

 35. Rubies for Gryffindor, sapphires for Ravenclaw,

emeralds for Slytherin. The stones used for Hufflepuff are never named, and the fact that gemstones are used in the hourglasses at all is mentioned significantly later than their first introduction in *Harry Potter and the Sorcerer's Stone*.

 36. 142 (HP1, chapter 8).

TRIVIA TIDBIT

BOOK VERSUS MOVIE

The moving staircases found in the Harry Potter films are not actually a feature of Hogwarts as J. K. Rowling describes it, unless you count the escalator-like spiral staircase leading to the headmaster's office. J. K. Rowling does state in her initial description of the castle that its rooms and other contents are not always fixed in place and that the staircases do at times lead to different destinations. The shifting staircases that clearly alter their destinations at whim are the film interpretation of that description, but the book version of Hogwarts never describes anyone watching or experiencing a staircase shift. Certainly, in either case, it must make getting to classes on time extremely difficult.

37. Over 100 (HP4, chapter 12). This is the largest number in any residence within wizarding England.

38. Pixies hung Neville Longbottom by the ears from an iron chandelier in the Defense Against the Dark Arts classroom. The chandelier did not survive this rough treatment, and has, to our knowledge, not yet been replaced (HP2, chapter 6).

39. To gain access to the kitchens at Hogwarts, which are located in the Great Hall, you have to tickle the pear in the bowl of fruit painting. The pear giggles before turning into a door handle (HP4, chapter 21).

40. The Sorting Hat is repeatedly mentioned as residing in Dumbledore's office, but whether it is a full-time resident there is unclear.

41. Eight. Seven, according to the Marauder's Map (HP3, chapter 10) and the passage to Hog's Head (HP7, chapter 29). There may be more, currently unknown.

42. Behind a mirror on the fourth floor of the castle. The Weasley Twins were using the passage, but had to give up on it (HP3, chapter 10).

43. Haunted, despite having been quiet (and unused by Remus Lupin for his werewolf transformations) for over twenty years (HP3, chapter 10).

44. Beech (HP1, chapter 13), oak (HP1, chapter 15), sycamore (HP2, chapter 15), yew (HP5, chapter 21), pine (HP5, chapter 30).

45. Each participant sings the Hogwarts song to his/her own preferred tune, inevitably creating a cacophony. In addition to Dumbledore, the Weasley Twins seemed particularly enamored with this tradition (HP1, chapter 7).

46. Through the blackboard. Ghosts, after all, don't need doors (HP2, chapter 9).

47. The Whomping Willow's violence can only be stopped on a temporary basis by touching a particular knot on it. Luckily, this can be done with a long stick, and does not require one to approach within range of extreme danger. Stunning spells and the like do not seem to work on the tree (HP3, chapter 10).

48. A secret passage leading out of Hogwarts and into the cellar at Honeydukes' (HP3, chapter 10).

49. 8 p.m. (HP4, chapter 20).

50. Moaning Myrtle's tantrums flooded it (HP1, chapter 8).

51. Salazar Slytherin felt that only pure-bloods should receive magical training at Hogwarts, an idea with which the other three founders disagreed (HP2, chapter 9).

52. Hogsmeade (HP3, chapter 1).

53. You need a note from a teacher, or the good luck not to open a particularly noisy book if you're there without permission (HP1, chapter 12). While the Restricted Section is blocked off with a rope, it does not seem to have any particular magic that prevents the section from being entered. Such magic is probably not necessary due to the tendency of the books located there to scream or otherwise act out in a way that would alert the professors and caretakers of the school.

54. Apollyon Pringle was Filch's equally, or perhaps more, severe predecessor. When he punished Arthur Weasley for being out with Molly after hours, he apparently left permanent scars (HP4, chapter 31).

55. *The Standard Book of Spells*. There is one for each grade. Harry purchased *The Standard Book of Spells Grade 1* for his first year (HP1, chapter 5), and the later grades of the books were mentioned throughout the series. We know there are at least six books in the series. Because we didn't see much of Hogwarts in *Harry Potter and the Deathly Hallows* we can't be sure there was a seventh (HP1, chapter 5).

56. Merpeople, Grindylows and the Giant Squid. Note that Merpeople fall into many categories, but it is only in the Mediterranean Sea that mermaids can be found (FB), and, as such, they do not count as a valid answer to this question.

57. An entire drawer of Filch's files is reserved for the antics of Fred and George Weasley (HP1, chapter 8).

58. Three (HP1, chapter 5).

59. In a cabinet in Filch's office labeled "Confiscated and Highly Dangerous" (HP3, chapter 10).

60. Twenty-eight (HP5, chapter 28).

61. Draco Malfoy (HP3, chapter 16).

62. Wilbert Slinkhard (HP5, chapter 9).

63. She could fire any teacher that wasn't, in her opinion, up to Ministry standards (HP5, chapter 26).

64. Apparition within the boundaries of Hogwarts is, at best, a bad idea. While House-elves seem to be able to do something of the sort (it looks the same even if the magic isn't), and like most things in the wizarding world there tend to be exceptions to every rule, apparition does not technically work inside of Hogwarts.

65. Fred, but to Ron's credit, he thought it was a lie (HP1, chapter 7).

66. Some bad experiences in fieldwork involving Hags and Vampires (HP1, chapter 5).

67. Eight (HP1, chapter 5).

68. Owls, cats or toads (HP1, chapter 5). Please note that a frog is not a toad.

69. Quentin Trimble (HP1, chapter 5).

70. July 31st for the term starting on September 1st (HP1, chapter 4).

71. Assuming you were not confused by the similarly titled *Defensive Magical Theory*, *Magical Theory* was authored by Adalbert Waffling (HP1, chapter 5).

72. Silver (HP1, chapter 5).

73. Madam Malkin's Robes for All Occasions (HP1, chapter 5).

74. First years are brought up from the train station by boats (holding no more than four students) across the lake (HP1, chapter 6). Older students take the carriages drawn by Thestrals (HP5, chapter 10).

75. Five (HP1, chapter 4).

QUEST 2
SPELLS & POTIONS

S pells and potions are at the core of what makes life in the wizarding world different from life in the Muggle world. The well-trained witch or wizard uses magic in all the most basic aspects of their lives. These include cooking and cleaning; health and medicine; communication and transportation; and safety, security and self-defense. In short, magic in the wizarding world may be even more pervasive than electricity is in the Muggle one.

In this Quest your knowledge will be tested on the formal lessons in magic you may have received. Questions here will address spells and charms, potions and plants and, in general, the knowledge you certainly never should have left Hogwarts without. Just everyday magic, which you probably picked up outside of an academic context, will be discussed later.

A Dragon designation awaits those who dance through these difficult questions, but if you remain perplexed, Phoenix will perhaps suit you best, and if you've just started your studies perhaps it is Salamander that will be your best buddy.

THE QUESTIONS

1. Against which creature would you use *Riddikulus*?

2. What is necessary to produce a Patronus?

3. How must asphodel be prepared for its inclusion in the Draught of Living Death?

4. A bezoar is of use under what circumstances?

5. What is the most effective way to get juice from sopophorous beans?

6. What does *Waddiwasi* do?

HINTS!

Hermione knew the answer to this question in her first Potions class, but Snape didn't let her answer because he was far more interested in berating Harry for the fact that he didn't know.

7. Deflating Draught is used when one has been affected by which potion?

8. From where is Instant Darkness Powder imported?

9. What are the ingredients of Polyjuice Potion?

10. How long does Polyjuice last?

11. What is commonly used as a thickening ingredient for potions?

12. Name the ingredients in Wit-Sharpening Potion.

HiNTS!

There are several places in the series to find the Polyjuice Potion ingredients. The necessity of Harry, Ron and Hermione, as well as the fake Moody, stealing some of the ingredients from Snape make the topic come up over and over again.

13. Name the main side effect of Pepperup Potion.

14. What ingredient did the Half-Blood Prince use to improve the Elixir to Induce Euphoria?

15. How much should you expect to pay for black beetle eyes?

16. What is the problem with consuming Unicorn blood?

17. What stench is emitted by the bubotuber?

18. What are the ingredients in the boil-curing potion?

HINTS!

A scoop of black beetle eyes is generally quite cheap, costing approximately a sixth of a Sickle. How many Knuts would that be?

19. What is one of the first charms a student learns at Hogwarts?

20. The Weasley twins are unavailable; how do you make something explode?

21. What incantation is used in executing a Summoning Charm?

22. Describe the wand movements for the charm in question 19.

23. How does the Fidelius Charm work?

24. Which potion requires a rat spleen as an ingredient?

HINTS!

The incantation used in this charm comes from the Latin meaning to send for or summon.

25. What are the incantations for the three Unforgivable Curses?

26. Describe the process of making an Unbreakable Vow.

27. *Anapneo* is used for what purpose?

28. Name the spells that can be used to breathe underwater.

29. Which charm did Lockhart use against the Pixies?

30. Which spell would you use to read invisible ink?

HINTS!

The spell Lockhart used probably wasn't a real one. In any case, it didn't work. If you were going to make up a spell to defeat fearsome Pixies, what would you call it?

31. Which spell is used for disarming?

32. Name the spells invented by the Half-Blood Prince.

33. If you can't afford an Invisibility Cloak, what would you treat a more mundane cloak with to have a similar effect?

34. What is presumably Lockhart's favorite charm?

35. Fiendfyre can destroy Horcruxes; what's the downside?

36. Which spell is used to produce the Dark Mark?

HINTS!

Fiendfyre is dangerous because it's more than just ordinary fire and can hunt down and destroy a lot more than Horcruxes. Explaining this magical fire's behavior answers the question.

37. Describe the appearance of mandrake roots.

38. How do you make a Portkey?

39. Who invented the Entrail-Expelling Curse?

40. Describe the two scenarios in which the prior spells cast by a given wand are displayed.

41. What factors are involved in the proper brewing of any potion?

42. What does *Ferula* do?

HINTS!

There is no one place to look for this answer. Rather, to get this question right you need to consider the various steps in potions preparation demonstrated in Snape's and Slughorn's classes.

43. Which store would you go to in order to acquire ingredients for a potion involving dark magic?

44. What is the correct color for the Shrinking Solution?

45. Which spell would necessitate the use of a boil cure potion?

46. Where would you find the feathers necessary to make both memory potions and truth serums?

47. In which type of potion are Ashwinder eggs of use?

48. Describe the differences between Gemino and *Geminio*.

Hints!

The potions Ashwinder eggs are best used for are not, on the surface, harmful, but can cause grave chaos, as Ron Weasley, having been the target of one, learned first hand at one point.

49. What are the three D's of Apparition?

50. How many uses of Dragon's blood are there?

51. Which spell would you use to detect any people that might be lurking in the immediate area?

52. The Sorcerer's Stone produces what potion?

53. Which spell did Harry use to conquer the first task in the Triwizard Tournament?

54. Who wrote *Defensive Magical Theory*?

HINTS!

The spell Harry used was not used against the Dragon of the first task. Rather, Harry used it to get the tool that allowed him to capture the egg.

55. What is the purpose of the spell Ron attempted (and failed at) on the Hogwarts Express on his way to his first year of school?

56. What is the supposed purpose of powdered Dragon claw?

57. Your latest Potions project has gone seriously wrong and you are beyond the help of the Hogwarts faculty. To which floor at St. Mungo's Hospital for Magical Ailments and Injuries should you report?

58. Aside from bans against a number of items, how does the W. E. A. ensure that there is no cheating on its exams?

59. What is the appropriate dosage of Veritaserum?

60. What do Centaurs use to enhance their stargazing?

Hints!

For a full accounting of the services available at St. Mungo's, and on which floor, best to look to the aftermath of Arthur Weasley's encounter with Nagini.

61. Name the commonly used cleaning charms.

62. When producing a Wit-Sharpening Potion what must you do to the scarab beetles?

63. What is the difference between the Animagus Transformation and a transfiguration into animal form?

64. Describe the effects of Impedimenta.

65. What curse did Sirius suggest as useful against Dragons?

66. Who wrote *One Thousand Magical Herbs and Fungi*?

HINTS!

While thinking will help you find the answer to any question, the way your thoughts work are especially relevant to the differences in these two transformations.

67. What does *Orchideous* do?

68. Name the two items in Harry's potions-making kit.

69. What does the Protean Charm do?

70. Who wrote *Advanced Potion-Making*?

71. What grouping of spells may not be used for punishment at Hogwarts?

72. What are the uses of scurvy-grass, lovage and sneezewort?

73. Describe the experience of drinking Skele-Gro.

74. What charm is used in Ton-Tongue Toffees?

75. Name the "latest revenges" according to Vindictus Viridian.

THE ANSWERS!

1. A boggart. This spell does not harm the boggart but rather eliminates its power to frighten, thus making it easy to subdue (HP3, chapter 7).

2. The caster must use the Patronus Charm while concentrating on a specific extremely happy memory (HP3, chapter 12).

3. It must be infused in wormwood (HP1, chapter 8).

TRIVIA TIDBIT

PLANTS: FACT & FICTION

Wormwood is another real plant that is both poisonous and medicinal depending on the usages and dosages involved. Wormwood is a prime ingredient in the drink absinthe, which has a long and controversial history and has often been blamed for a range of social ills. Additionally, wormwood has long been considered to be a remedy for stomach ailments.

4. A bezoar will act as an antidote to most poisons (HP1, chapter 8).

5. Sopophorus beans produce the most juice when crushed with the flat of a silver knife. These instructions come from the Half-Blood Prince as an improvement upon the instructions listed in the actual textbook (HP6, chapter 9).

6. Professor Lupin used *Waddiwasi* to remove a wad of chewing gum from a lock and direct it up the nose of the culprit who put it there. Predictably, the culprit was Peeves (HP3, chapter 7).

7. Swelling Solution (HP2, chapter 11).

8. Instant Darkness Powder was imported by the Weasley twins from Peru. This does not rule out the possibility that it may have other countries of origin as well (HP6, chapter 6).

9. Lacewing flies, leeches, bicorn horn, knotgrass, fluxweed, boomslang skin, and some small part (hair seems to be preferred) of the person you wish to be Polyjuiced into (HP2, chapters 10 and 11).

10. One hour, although one can continue to take more doses before reverting to one's true form without seeming to be harmed (HP2, chapter 12). That said, it's hard to tell if the ongoing use of Polyjuice negatively affected Barty Crouch, Jr. considering he was a fairly unbalanced and damaged individual before the ruse in which he masqueraded as legendary Auror, Mad-Eye Moody.

11. Fobberworm mucus (FB).

12. Armadillo bile, cut ginger roots and ground scarab beetle (HP4, chapter 27).

13. Pepperup Potion will cause the drinker to have smoke coming out of their ears for several hours (HP2, chapter 8).

14. Peppermint to counteract the side effects of singing and nose-tweaking (HP6, chapter 22).

15. Five Knuts per scoop, at least in the week before Harry's first year at Hogwarts (HP1, chapter 5). No current prices accounting for inflation and the possible economic results of the wizarding war are available.

16. While Unicorn blood can save the life of someone in dire circumstances, the quality of life it provides is hor-

rible. Drinking Unicorn blood curses the life it has been intended to save because one has chosen to kill something pure and utterly defenseless in the name of selfishness (HP1, chapter 15). Presumably this problem exists with blood taken from a wounded Unicorn as well.

17. That of gasoline (HP4, chapter 13).

18. Nettles, snake fangs, horned slugs, and porcupine quills (HP1, chapter 8).

19. The Levitation Charm, *Wingardium Leviosa* (HP1, chapter 10).

20. The fluid from an Erumpent's horn (FB), a *Confringo* spell (HP7, chapter 4) or *Expulso* (HP7, chapter 9). If you need to just make a significant hole in something as opposed to exploding the whole thing *Deprimo* might be a good choice as well (HP7, chapter 21).

21. *Accio* is generally used as a Summoning Charm. Mostly it is used on inanimate objects, but occasionally it is targeted at people or parts of people. This use of *Accio* is probably worthy of an essay in a wizarding ethics class, as such a use would theoretically interfere with the free will of the creature in question and possibly skirt dangerously close to the Imperius Curse.

22. "Swish and flick" (HP1, chapter 10).

 23. The Fidelius Charm is a way of keeping a piece of information secret by means of a "Secret-keeper." When this spell is performed a Secret-keeper is designated and that person becomes the only person capable of mentioning the secret in question. The Secret-keeper may divulge the secret to anyone who needs to know it, or, in fact, any person at all, making the selection of the Secret-keeper of vital importance. In the event of the Secret-keeper's death, each individual who was told the secret by the keeper is now also a Secret-keeper, thus weakening the power of the spell over time. The notion that the more people who know a secret, the less of a secret it is likely to remain is as true in the wizarding world as in the Muggle one. Details of the Fidelius Charm appear in Harry Potter books three through seven.

24. Shrinking Solution (HP3, chapter 7).

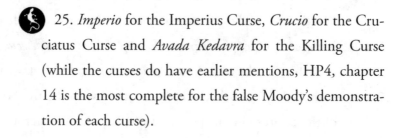 25. *Imperio* for the Imperius Curse, *Crucio* for the Cruciatus Curse and *Avada Kedavra* for the Killing Curse (while the curses do have earlier mentions, HP4, chapter 14 is the most complete for the false Moody's demonstration of each curse).

TRIVIA TIDBIT

MAGIC, MYTH & MUGGLES

Avada Kedavra is related to the commonly known magical word abracadabra which itself comes from an Aramaic phrase that is generally translated to command a thing to disappear or even be destroyed. J. K. Rowling spoke about these origins of the most feared curse in the wizarding world at the Edinburgh Book Festival in 2004. Crucio, meanwhile, means "I torture" in Latin. Similarly Imperio, while not proper Latin itself, comes from imperare, the verb meaning "to order."

26. The making of an Unbreakable Vow requires a third, essentially uninvolved individual, to cast the spell directly on the joined hands of the person making the vow and the person to whom the vow is being made (HP6, chapter 2). Vows may have multiple components and the spell seals each aspect of such a commitment.

27. Anapneo will clear a blocked airway. Consider it the magical equivalent of the Heimlich Maneuver (HP6, chapter 7).

28. The Bubble-Head Charm is the most effective spell for breathing under water or in any environment where fresh air is at a premium (HP4, chapter 26). A transfiguration into a creature that can breathe under water is also an option, although one that was not very effective for Viktor Krum in the second task at the Triwizard Tournament. Gillyweed, another solution for breathing underwater, is not a spell (it's not even a potion, rather it's just a plant in its natural state) and is therefore not a valid answer to this question.

29. Lockhart uses what he claims is a Freezing Charm, but we never see anyone else use this incantation (*Peskipiksi Pesternomi*), nor does it succeed, calling its legitimacy into question (HP2, chapter 6).

30. *Aparecium* (HP2, chapter 13).

31. *Expelliarmus* (HP2, chapter 10) is the disarming spell introduced to Harry's class. While this is called a disarming spell, the results seem to often be rather more severe than just removing the wand from the target individual.

32. *Sectumsempera* (HP6, chapter 21) and *Levicorpus* and *Liberacorpus* (HP6, chapter 12). It seems likely that Snape, both during and after his use of the Half-Blood

Prince persona, created other spells, but we do not know what they are.

33. The Disillusionment Charm or Bedazzling Hex would probably be your best choices (HP7, chapter 21). However, these would probably not render the user invisible so much as unlikely to be noticed or focused upon.

34. *Obliviate* is the Memory Charm cited constantly throughout the series as used by the Ministry on Muggles to help enforce the secrecy of the wizarding world. Lockhart is cited as having used Memory Charms on those whose life stories he stole for his books, and it is this same Memory Charm that backfires on him and eventually lands him in St. Mungo's Hospital (HP2, chapter 16).

35. Fiendfyre has several downsides. Its flames are exceptionally large and produce extreme heat. Additionally, fiendfyre left burning will take on the forms of Beasts, which will then pursue those designated as targets (HP7, chapter 31).

36. *Morsmordre* (HP4, chapter 9) produces the Dark Mark in the sky.

37. In the wizarding world, mandrake roots look like babies (HP2, chapter 6).

TRIVIA TIDBIT

PLANTS: FACT & FICTION

The real mandrake plant does have roots with a human-like appearance, but the figure is much less defined than that of the mandrakes of the wizarding world. The plant is poisonous and because of its unusual appearance has long captured the imagination. It appears in the Bible as well as in the works of Machiavelli, Shakespeare, Ezra Pound and Samuel Beckett, among many others.

38. The *Portus* spell is used on the object one wishes to turn into a Portkey. The creation of Portkeys is governed by the Ministry of Magic (HP5, chapter 22).

39. Urquhart Rackharrow (HP5, chapter 22).

40. The situation being described is that of *Piori Incantatem*. There are two ways to produce this effect. The first is the use of the spell *Priori Incantato*, which will cause the wand that is the target of the spell to emit a ghostly image of the last spell cast with it (HP4, chapter 9). It is unclear how many spells back this can be used to reveal. The

second way to produce *Priori Icantatem* requires that two wands with cores from the same creature (not just type of creature) face each other magically. In this scenario one wand will show the last spells cast from it. Which wand reveals this information is dependent upon the will and power of the wizards involved (HP4, chapter 36).

41. Potion ingredients must be prepared correctly (e.g., chopped roots will produce a different result from sliced roots) and added in the correct order. Additionally, application of heat as well as direction and frequency of stirring must also be executed with precision. These keys to effective potion brewing are made clear throughout the potion lessons both Snape and Slughorn present in the course of the books.

42. *Ferula* creates a wooden rod or stick (HP3, chapter 19). It seems unlikely that wands count in this category since we do not see any use of it in the many confrontations in which wizards lose theirs on even a temporary basis.

43. You might want to check in Borgin & Burkes, which focuses on dark magic in general more than potions in specific. But if you're looking for a dark, cursed or not strictly legal item, it seems they can probably help (HP2, chapter 4).

44. Green (HP3, chapter 7).

45. *Furnunculus* (HP2, chapter 11).

46. On the Jobberknoll (FB).

47. Love Potions (FB).

48. *Geminio* duplicates whatever the spell is aimed at (HP7, chapter 13). On the other hand, the Gemino Curse causes an object to duplicate worthlessly every time it is touched. This is used as a security measure at Gringotts since it threatens thieves with being crushed or drowned by fake gold (HP7, chapter 26).

49. "Destination, Determination and Deliberation" (HP6, chapter 18).

50. Twelve, and while Dumbledore discovered them, he never tells us what they are (HP1, chapter 6) although it is clear that Hogwarts students are taught them.

51. Homenum revelio (HP7, chapter 9).

52. The Sorcerer's (or Philosopher's depending on your edition) Stone is the source of the Elixir of Life. It is un-clear whether this fluid comes directly from the Stone or

if the Stone is merely used in making the potion (HP1, chapter 13).

TRIVIA TIDBIT

MAGIC, MYTH & MUGGLES

In alchemy, a term for both an early form of science and a philosophical discipline linked to it that has existed for thousands of years, the philosopher's stone was viewed as the ultimate achievement. If created, it was believed not only to hold the power to turn base metals into gold but also to counteract aging.

---

53. Harry used *Accio* to retrieve his broom as a method for evading the Dragon and completing the first task (HP4, chapter 20).

54. Wilbert Slinkhard (HP5, chapter 9).

55. Ron tried to turn Scabbers yellow via a rhyming spell George supplied to him. It didn't work and both he and Hermione doubted its validity as a spell (HP1, chapter 6).

56. Powdered Dragon claw, according to Ron and apparently Harold Dingle, will boost your brainpower and cleverness for several hours. Hermione insisted this was not effective, especially in the case of Dingle who was actually only in possession of dried doxy droppings (HP5, chapter 31).

57. The third floor (HP5, chapter 21).

58. Anti-Cheating Charms (HP5, chapter 31).

59. Three drops are, according to Snape, incredibly effective. Whether this is the necessary, maximum, or even ideal dose is unclear (HP4, chapter 27).

60. Mallowsweet (HP5, chapter 27).

61. There are actually several commonly used cleaning charms including Tergeo (HP6, chapter 8) and the Scouring Charm (HP4, chapter 14) which may or may not be the same charm as *Scourgify* (HP5, chapter 3) that also has a cleaning effect.

62. The scarab beetles must be ground using a mortar and pestle (HP4, chapter 27). Harry is described, however, as mashing them, which may not be precisely the same

thing for potions purposes.

63. The difference between an Animagus Transformation and a regular transfiguration is that that Animagus Transformation allows the witch or wizard to retain human intelligence and values. The Animagus Transformation seems to happen wandlessly whereas transfigurations generally require the wand as a focusing tool.

64. *Impedimenta* is a binding spell. When used people seem to be bound by invisible ropes. It is not as secure as *Perfectus Totalis* because we see that the target is able to struggle against these invisible chains and overcome them to some degree, as in the case of Snape when James casts it on him in the memory Harry views in the Pensieve (HP5, chapter 28).

65. The Conjunctivitis Curse (HP4, chapter 19).

66. Phyllida Spore (HP1, chapter 5).

67. As is commonly seen in Muggle versions of illusion-based magic, *Orchideous* causes a bouquet of flowers to be produced from the end of a wand (HP4, chapter 18).

68. Spine of lionfish and essence of belladonna (HP4,

chapter 10) are listed as two ingredients in Harry's potions-making kit that he needs to refill before he begins his fourth year at Hogwarts.

TRIVIA TIDBIT

PLANTS: FACT & FICTION

Belladonna is a real and poisonous plant also known as deadly nightshade. It can cause blistering and other skin reactions upon contact and is harmful to a wide range of animals, including humans. Belladonna also has a number of medicinal purposes and in small doses is a part of several modern medicines.

69. The Protean Charm allows objects designed for one purpose to be used for another such as the message transmitting coins that Hermione (HP5, chapter 19) and later Draco (HP7, chapter 27) created. Hermione was apparently inspired by the way Voldemort was able to communicate with his followers via the Dark Mark, but it is unclear whether the Charm was a part of the magic contained in those marks.

TRIVIA TIDBIT

MAGIC, MUGGLES & MYTH

In ancient Greek mythology Proteus was a sea god known for changing shape to evade capture. This becomes particularly clear in Homer's *Odyssey* when Proteus took the form of a series of Beasts to evade capture by Menelaus. This, however, was not successful and while in capture, Proteus was required to tell the truth; just as the coins Hermione treated with the charm did after somewhat less dramatic changes in form.

70. Libatius Borage (HP6, chapter 9).

71. After the false Moody briefly turned Draco into a ferret, we learn from McGonogal's shocked reaction that transfigurations are never suitable for punishing students (HP4, chapter 13).

72. They are all ingredients in the Confusing and Befuddlement Draught (HP5, chapter 18).

TRIVIA TIDBIT

PLANTS: FACT & FICTION

Lovage is commonly used to flavor food, and tea made from it can also be used as an antiseptic or to soothe the stomach. It is related to celery and is praised as a "companion plant" generally improving the health of plants it grows near.

73. Unlike much of the magical healing we see in the wizarding world, Skele-Gro is clearly painful. The sensation of bones regenerating causes stabbing pain and the potion itself burns the mouth when consumed (HP2, chapter 10). This serves as a valuable reminder to both Harry and the reader that the wizarding world is far from free of the physical risks and pains of the Muggle one.

74. An Engorgement Charm (HP4, chapter 4).

75. Hair loss, jelly legs and tongue tying (HP1, chapter 5) and apparently that's just the beginning!

QUEST 3

THE MAGICAL MENAGERIE

B eing able to identify the myriad members of the magical menagerie is a critical skill for every witch and wizard and, of course, of great interest to the curious Muggle as well. Without an understanding of the differences between Beasts and Beings or creatures like Fairies, Doxies and Imps, a witch or wizard runs not only the risk of creating an international incident, but also of putting themselves and their household in serious danger.

If you are alive to answer the questions in this Quest, chances are you have never met a Basilisk, Erumpent or Manticore in person. But that is no reason not to know about them! After all, knowledge, while not necessarily as effective as a good stunning spell, is often your best defense.

Do you know enough about Dragons to receive a Dragon rating on this Quest? Or do you remember so few features about these creatures as to merely be classified as a Phoenix? And if some of the similarities between these strange specimens stymie you, then perhaps Salamander is the best you'll do!

THE QUESTIONS

1. What is a Grindylow?

2. What was the Ilfracombe Incident of 1932?

3. What is the weakest part of a Dragon?

4. Who is the author of *Fantastic Beasts and Where to Find Them*?

5. When did the Ban on Experimental Breeding go into effect?

6. Name the ten non-hybrid breeds of Dragon.

HINTS!

This author's name is made up of a name that can be shortened to a creature that exists in both the Muggle and wizarding worlds, the name of an ancient Greek goddess, a common name for a dog and something that sounds suspiciously like this level of question.

7. How many heads does Fluffy have?

8. What is the typical herd size of the Centaur?

9. When was Clause 73 inserted into the International Code of Wizarding Secrecy?

10. Which potion is used to treat Werewolves?

11. Which Ministry department handles dangerous creatures that require extreme measures?

12. On which continents does the Dugbog live?

HINTS!

Buckbeak's planned and failed execution was handled by this Ministry division.

13. How many eyes does the Acromantula have?

14. What precautions must be taken when owning a Fwooper?

15. How does one create a Basilisk?

16. To which continent is the Billywig native?

17. What do Muggles believe the Diricawl to be?

18. Describe the differences between the male and female Blast-Ended Skrewt.

HINTS!

If Muggles can no longer see an animal they were once familiar with, are they more likely to assume powers or invisibility or extinction. If you chose invisibility, you must have flunked your Muggle Studies class.

19. Name the components of the Chimaera.

20. What was the Augurey originally believed to foretell and what does it actually foretell instead?

21. What is the Hippocampus?

22. What are the requirements for seeing a Thestral?

23. Describe the life-cycle of the Fairy.

24. On the subject of which magical creature do Severus Snape and Newt Scamander disagree?

HINTS!

Harry thinks these creatures are invisible until his encounter with Voldemort at the end of the Triwizard tournament.

25. Where is the world's largest, and perhaps most fa-mous, Kelpie located?

26. Name the components of a Cockatrice.

27. Describe the life-cycle of the Ashwinder.

28. Name the components of the Manticore.

29. What does the Erkling like to eat?

30.Name the four breeds of winged horse.

HINTS!

Perhaps this will help refresh your memory. The Ashwinder lives briefly, burns brightly and is created, generally, by a negligent wizard or one looking for a certain very valuable potion ingredient.

31. Name the three types of Trolls.

32. What is probably the most dangerous Beast of all?

33. What is an alternate name for the Leprechaun?

34. What is a Kneazle?

35. What is the proper way to greet a Hippogriff?

36. When Dragon hide isn't enough, what creature's hide will offer a witch or wizard even more protection?

HINTS!

Considering the type of courtesy that Hippogriffs demand, you would think Draco Malfoy, who surely should have had etiquette lessons from his snobbish family, would have done a better job of greeting him.

37. What Muggle pet does the Crup resemble?

38. What fungus-like creature can destroy a house or clean it depending on whether its secretions have been diluted or not?

39. Name two creatures that can help you get rid of Horklumps.

40. Chameleon Ghouls are known to take the form of what object common to Hogwarts?

41. What is a Grim?

42. Describe the differences between the Imp and the Pixie.

HiNTS!

Horklumps are annoying Beasts. Unfortunately, so is one of the creatures that likes to feast on them.

43. What is the Dementor's Kiss?

44. To which part of the world is the Re'em native?

45. Albino bloodhounds are of use in combating which creature?

46. What is unusual about Fleur Delacour's ancestry?

47. Why is the Occamy particularly defensive of its eggs?

48. Why was the Isle of Drear made unplottable?

Hints!

The Occamy may not be the goose that laid the golden egg, but its eggs have a particular and somewhat similar value to make them fiercely desired by many.

49. What is a secondary name for the Doxy?

 50. What is the proper name of the creature commonly known as "the living shroud?"

 51. Name all the known water demons.

 52. Name the two creatures that would have status as Beings except for the fact that they requested classification as Beasts.

 53. Why is the Lobalug used as a weapon?

 54. How much do Unicorn horns cost?

HiNTS!

Both of the creature types to have shunned "Being" status live on the Hogwarts property – one in the lake and one in the forest.

55. Name the centaurs of the Forbidden Forest.

56. Why is Moke skin valuable?

57. What is the preferred drink of the winged horse?

58. How can you tell if the Clabbert thinks itself in danger?

59. What is the paranoid magical equivalent of a hedgehog?

60. How does the magic of House-elves differ from that of humans?

61. Invisibility cloaks may be made out of the hair of which creature?

62. What is the purpose of the Porlock?

63. Although the Jarvey can speak, it is still classified as a Beast. Why?

64. What species of Dragon is Norbert?

65. Name the three Ministry departments that handle Werewolf issues.

66. How are Werewolves, Hags and Vampires classified by the Ministry?

67. When seeking material from a tree inhabited by a Bowtruckle, what is the best way to proceed?

68. What do Murtlaps eat other than crustaceans?

69. Which Minister of Magic came up with the current guidelines used to determine Beast or Being status?

HINTS!

Crustaceans are creatures that live on the floors of lakes and oceans. This closeness to the floor is a common trait shared by all of the things Murtlaps dine on. What is the other item?

70. Describe the Sphinx.

71. When it was first agreed to hide some magical Beasts from the eyes of Muggles, how many types of creatures were originally included as subjects of the decision?

72. When did the creation of Basilisks become illegal?

73. How many classification levels does the Ministry use to describe a creature's danger level?

74. Where did the earliest documented Lethifold attack take place?

75. What does one feed a newly hatched Dragon?

THE ANSWERS !

1. The Grindylow is a water demon found in British and Irish lakes and occasionally domesticated by Merpeople (HP3, chapter 8; FB).

2. A Dragon swooped down on a Muggle beach, requiring the performance of the largest known batch of Memory Charms in the 20th century; Gilderoy Lockhart was not involved (FB).

3. The eyes (HP4, chapter 23).

4. Newton "Newt" Artemis Fido Scamander (HP1, chapter 5; FB).

5. The ban went into effect in 1965 (FB), but this does not seem to have stopped Hagrid, among others.

6. Antipodean Opaleye, Chinese Fireball (LionDragon is also an acceptable term for this breed), Common Welsh Green, Hebridean Black, Hungarian Horntail, Norwegian Ridgeback, Peruvian Vipertooth, Romanian Longhorn,

Swedish Short-Snout, and the Ukranian Ironbelly (FB). These Dragons are, of course, introduced to us throughout the series, particularly in *Goblet of Fire*.

TRIVIA TIDBIT

MAGIC, MYTH & MUGGLES

Dragons exist in mythology around the world. Their characteristics differ depending on their country and particular myth of origin. Some, but not all, breathe fire, and while some are benevolent, many are not. Dragons also may or may not have wings, feathers or multiple heads depending on their provenance and purpose.

7. Fluffy, one of the obstacles guarding the Sorcerer's Stone, has three heads (HP1, chapter 9).

TRIVIA TIDBIT

MAGIC, MYTH & MUGGLES

In ancient Greek and Roman mythology, Cerberus is a three-headed hound that guarded the gates of the underworld to make sure that only the dead and not the living entered the realm and to make sure that none could leave. Cerberus is not unlike Fluffy insomuch that there were ways to sneak past him and people did, at least occasionally; Orpheus lulled him to sleep with music, and at various other times the fierce dog was drugged or wrestled into submission, implying that it may not have been poor singing skills but another strategy gone awry that caused Fluffy to bite Snape.

 8. Ten to fifty (FB).

 9. 1750 (FB).

10. The Wolfsbane potion (HP3, chapter 18). This potion does not cure lycanthropy or prevent the transformation, but allows the human in wolf form to retain reason and therefore, presumably, not infect or otherwise harm others.

TRIVIA TIDBIT

POISONOUS PLANTS

In addition to being the name of the potion administered to Werewolves in the wizarding world, Wolfsbane is one of many names of an extremely poisonous and perfectly real plant that is also known as aconite and, because of its appearance, monkshood. Professor Snape quizzed Harry on these alternate names at the trio's first potions class (HP1, chapter 8).

11. The Committee for the Disposal of Dangerous Creatures (HP3, chapter 11).

12. The Dugbog can be found in Europe and the Americas (FB).

13. Eight (FB).

14. The Fwooper's song, while enjoyable, can induce insanity. As such, owning a Fwooper requires a license and a silencing charm on the bird which must be renewed monthly (FB).

15. The Basilisk is created by hatching a chicken egg under a toad (FB).

TRIVIA TIDBIT

MAGIC, MYTH & MUGGLES

In legend the Basilisk is said to be the king of the serpents. It is sometimes also called a Cockatrice, although the two creatures are not consistently described as one and the same. In the Muggle world, Basilisk is the name given to a genus of lizard and one member of this family, the green or plumed Basilisk, can run on the surface of water.

---

16. Australia (FB).

17. Thanks to its ability to disappear and reappear, Muggles believe the Diricawl to be the extinct Dodo.

TRIVIA TIDBIT

MAGIC, MYTH & MUGGLES

There is nothing mythical about the Dodo (Raphus cucullatus) unless someone reports seeing this creature, which has been extinct for several centuries, alive. The flightless bird was native to Mauritius and its extinction seems to have been driven by non-native animals introduced to Mauritius by humans.

18. Only Rubeus Hagrid knows the answer to this question for sure (well, presumably the Screwts know as well), as he is the one who bred these illegal hybrids. He theorized that the Screwts with stingers were male and those with suckers in their bodies that fed on blood were the females (HP4, chapter 13).

19. The Chimaera has the head of a lion, the body of a goat, and the tail of a Dragon (FB).

TRIVIA TIDBIT

MAGIC, MYTH & MUGGLES

In Greek mythology, the Chimera was a single creature born to Typhone and Echidna. She was a sibling both to the Cerberus and the Hydra of Lerna, but in the world of Harry Potter, chimaeras refer to an entire species of magical creature. In American spelling generally "chimaera" with an "ae" is only used to refer to a genus of fish sometimes also called "ghost sharks." Chimera is also a frequently used term in science and genetics.

20. The Augurey's call was believed to foretell death, but eventually it became clear that the only thing it actually signals is rain (FB).

21. The Hippocampus has the head and front legs of a horse and the tail of a giant fish (FB).

22. Having seen death (HP5, chapter 21).

TRIVIA TIDBIT

MAGIC, MYTH & MUGGLES

While "hippocampus" is the Latin name for a mythological sea horse, it is also a genus of the real world and much smaller seahorse and a term for the part of the brain so named due to its shape.

23. Fairies hatch from eggs as larvae. At approximately one week old they form a cocoon in which they spend a month before emerging as the winged adults. Fairies lay as many as fifty eggs at once time.

24. In *Fantastic Beasts and Where to Find Them* Newt Scamander lists Japan as the home of the Kappa (FB). However, Professor Snape said they are generally found in Mongolia (HP1, chapter 9). Considering the useful notations Snape (in the guise of the Half-Blood Prince) left in the book Harry wound up using as his sixth year potions text, which wizard is correct may be considered impossible to ascertain without travel to the areas in question. However, because the Kappa is a water creature and Mongolia is mostly a desert, this one may have to be awarded to Scamander.

TRIVIA TIDBIT

MAGIC, MYTH & MUGGLES

Muggle mythology agrees with Newt Scamander on the subject of the Kappa's location, and this water sprite may be better known than you realize. Kappa maki, the cucumber roll you may have eaten at a sushi restaurant, is so named because the cucumber is an especially beloved meal for the Kappa, also particularly fond of eating children.

If you don't have any cucumbers handy, Muggle mythologists agree with wizards and recommend bowing to the creatures should you encounter one. When the Kappa returns the bow the liquid that fills the bowl-like depression in their heads will flow out, weakening them and forcing them back into the water.

 25. Loch Ness (FB).

Trivia Tidbit

Magic, Myth & Muggles

For all the Muggle world knows, the legendary Loch Ness Monster, if it exists, may in fact be a kelpie. But it may also be an optical illusion, an as yet unknown species, a species believed to be extinct or a common species that has somehow been misidentified as something highly unusual.

Regardless of her status, the Loch Ness Monster, also known as Nessie, is extraordinarily popular amongst Muggles; she even has her own website documenting sightings of the creature both on land and in the water.

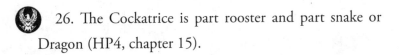 26. The Cockatrice is part rooster and part snake or Dragon (HP4, chapter 15).

Trivia Tidbit

Magic, Myth & Muggles

Cockatrice is generally, but not exclusively, considered to be the Elizabethan name for the Basilisk. It was believed that its gaze would kill or at least turn to stone whatever looked at it, making it especially problematic to destroy. Only the weasel was said to be immune. It was generally considered to be the product of a chicken egg hatched by a serpent, toad or other reptile, giving it both powers and origins similar to that of the Basilisk.

27. The Ashwinder is another of the magical species requiring some action on the part of a witch or wizard for its creation. Ashwinders emerge from untended magical fires, and despite living for just an hour, are a significant hazard because their eggs can quickly ignite a building if they are not found and frozen (FB).

28. The Manticore has a man's head, a lion's body and a scorpion's tail (FB).

29. Children (FB).

TRIVIA TIDBIT

MAGIC, MYTH & MUGGLES

Manticores appear frequently in both myth and ancient science originating in Persia and the Roman empire. Today they remain common in literature, even appearing in the works of Salman Rushdie. Manticores also remain a powerful legend in Indonesia where they are said to inhabit forests. In the wizarding world, however, the Manticore is classified as a creature of strictly Greek origin (FB).

30. Winged horse breeds include Abraxan, Aethonan, Granian and Thestral (FB).

31. Mountain, forest and river (FB).

32. The Nundu is probably the most dangerous Beast on the planet. Its breath causes a disease that can wipe out an entire village. Because of its large size and ability to move silently, it has never been subdued by less than a hundred wizards working together (FB).

33. The Leprechaun is also known as the Clauricorn (FB).

TRĪVĪA TĪDBĪT

MAGĪC, MYTH & MUGGLES

Perhaps the most famous winged horse of all is Pegasus from Greek mythology. There are many variations in the story of the birth and life of Pegasus, but he is generally considered to have aided the hero Bellerophon in the slaying of the Chimera. Zeus is said to have later honored Pegasus with a constellation, which can be seen in the night sky even today.

34. The Kneazle is a cat-like creature that is very fond of wizards and rather unfond of Muggles. They are also reputed to be quite intelligent (FB).

35. Hippogriffs are formal creatures that must be dealt with respectfully. The person making the approach must maintain eye contact and bow to the creature before attempting to touch it. If the Hippogriff responds to the bow in kind, the person can then attempt further interaction with the Beast, such as petting or riding it. The Hippogriff does not take well to insults (HP3, chapter 5).

36. Hide from the Graphorn, which is large enough for a Troll to ride atop (and sometimes they do!), is even stronger than Dragon hide (FB).

37. The Crup resembles the Jack Russell Terrier, except that it has a forked tail and an appetite like a goat (FB).

38. Bundimuns look like fungus but are not, since they do actually have legs and eyes. Their secretions, which are used in diluted form in household cleaning products, are powerful enough in their pure form to destroy a house by causing its foundations to rot (FB).

39. Streelers' venom is harmful to Horklumps, and Gnomes enjoy them as food. Of course, the Streeler remedy to the problem is recommended as Streelers are often kept as pets, but most wizards and witches view Gnomes as pests (FB).

40. Suits of armor (HP2, chapter 10).

41. The Grim is not technically a Beast at all; it is not a living creature, but rather a portent of death that looks like a large spectral dog (HP3, chapter 6).

42. Imps and Pixies differ in aspects of appearance, behavior, life cycle and location. The Imp cannot fly while

the Pixie can; the Imp is generally blackish in color as opposed to electric blue; the Imp hatches young from eggs while Pixies have live births; the Imp lives throughout Britain and Ireland, whereas the Pixie mostly keeps to Cornwall (FB).

TRIVIA TIDBIT

MAGIC, MYTH & MUGGLES

The pixies of myth and legend are also generally said to hail from Cornwall and are known as tricksters. It is said they can be repelled by iron or placated with small gifts of food. Despite their legendary status, pixie sightings do occasionally appear in the Muggle media and online as in the case of a series of mishaps during the construction of the Hinkley Point nuclear power station in Somerset, England.

43. The Dementor's Kiss is the most horrible of the many horrible things dementors do. When the dementor delivers its kiss it actually consumes the soul of the person in question, leaving them a living, breathing husk without personality or volition (HP5, chapter 12).

44. The Re'em is native to both North America and the

Far East (FB).

TRIVIA TIDBIT

MAGIC, MYTH & MUGGLES

The Re'em is a creature of Jewish mythology and is also mentioned repeatedly in the Bible where it has been translated at various points as both "unicorn" and "wild ox." Because of the creature's massive size only two of them – a male and a female – were said to exist at one time because the earth would not otherwise be able to support their weight. Their mass was also an issue for Noah, and various legends exist about how he saved them from the Flood; it is often suggested that they were tethered to the ark and swam behind it.

45. The Nogtail can be chased permanently from a farm it is plaguing by a pure white dog. The dog does not, technically, have to be an albino bloodhound, but they do make the task easier (FB).

46. Fleur is part Veela through a grandmother who provided the core for her wand in the form of a hair (HP4, chapter 18).

47. The Occamy's eggs are silver, making them a particularly interesting target for thieves (FB).

48. The Isle of Drear is the only home of Quintapeds, carnivorous creatures that prefer human flesh (FB).

49. The Doxy is also known as the biting fairy (FB).

50. The Lethifold is the creature also known as the living shroud (FB).

51. Grindylows, Kappas and Kelpies are the three known forms of water demons (FB).

52. Both the Centaurs and the Merpeople, despite being eligible to be classified as Beings, have requested to remain Beasts (FB).

53. The Lobalug is little more than a poison pouch with a spout attached. At slightly less than a foot long, it is easy to carry and quite dangerous, making it useful as a weapon to the Merpeople. Whether it can be used in this way outside of a watery environment is not known, although its poison may be used as a potion ingredient (FB).

54. Twenty-one Galleons each in Diagon Alley in 1991 (HP1, chapter 5). We do not have any current information on how inflation and the wizarding war may have affected this price.

55. Since Centaurs largely prefer to keep to their own kind, we only know the names of four of the Forbidden Forest centaurs, despite the size of their herd. These known centaurs are Bane, Firenze and Ronan (HP1, chapter 15) and Magorian (HP5, chapter 30).

56. The Moke is a lizard that can shrink at will, often in response to perceived danger. Its skin will continue to behave like this even after it is removed from the creature, making it an ideal material for moneybags and other pouches that are at risk from thieves (FB).

57. Single-malt whiskey (HP4, chapter 15).

58. The Clabbert has a pustule on the center of its forehead that flashes red when it senses itself to be in danger (FB).

59. The Knarl is a creature so paranoid that it presumes offers of food are a trick and attempts at kindness will usually result in the Knarl being destructive instead (FB).

60. Throughout the series we see that House-elves do not use wands or even words to focus their magic.

61. The Demiguise can make itself indivisible when threatened, and its silvery hair can be used to make Invisibility Cloaks (FB).

62. The Porlock guards horses. As it is shy and dislikes humans, it seems to do this of its own accord and would be a welcome addition to any stable (FB).

63. While the Jarvey can speak, the ability to speak is not enough to receive the classification of Being as opposed to Beast. A Being must be able to understand and participate in magical lawmaking. Jarveys, whose speech is limited almost entirely to insults, do not have that capability (FB).

64. A Norwegian Ridgeback (HP1, chapter 14).

65. The Werewolf Capture Unit, the Werewolf Registry and Werewolf Support Services (FB).

66. Hags and Vampires are classified as Beings. Werewolves have an unclear and indeterminate designation as the Ministry departments concerned with them are divided between Beast and Being divisions (FB). The status of werewolves in the wizarding world also shifts with the political winds as seen in the fortunes of Remus Lupin and the Werewolf alliance with Voldemort.

67. Because Bowtruckles regard themselves as the guardians of the trees they inhabit (generally those in parts of England, Germany and Scandinavia), it is best to appease or distract the creature before trying to harvest any material from its home tree. Luckily, woodlice seem to be particularly pleasing to it (FB).

68. The feet of people who step on them (FB).

69. Grogan Stump in 1811 (FB).

70. Sphinxes have a human head on a lion's body and a fondness for riddles (FB).

TRIVIA TIDBIT

MAGIC, MYTH & MUGGLES

The Sphinx appears throughout history and art in many forms. The ancient Egyptians portrayed three types of Sphinx all of which had a lion's body but the head of a person, a ram or a bird. In Ancient Greece the Sphinx was a singular creature that was defeated when Oedipus finally solved her riddle. Sphinxes also appear in various South Asian mythologies and have been revived periodically as themes in Western artwork.

71. Twenty-seven (FB).

 72. Newt Scamander does not supply us with a clear date on this matter, merely telling us that it happened at some point in the Middle Ages (FB).

73. Five, ranging from "Boring" to "Known Wizard Killer." The scale, unfortunately, is not entirely reliable. Some creatures are given a higher danger rating not because they are dangerous but because they must be treated with so much respect (FB). Additionally, the experiences of individual wizards may vary.

74. Papua New Guinea in 1782 (FB).

75. According to *Dragon Breeding for Pleasure and Profit,* a newly hatched Dragon should have a bucket of brandy mixed with chicken blood twice an hour (HP1, chapter 14).

QUEST 4

EVERYDAY MAGIC

S ome things you just can't learn in school, or at least, not in the actual classroom. The questions in this Quest focus on the knowledge you will have picked up just by being a part of the magical world. Jokes, trinkets, snacks and various enchanted objects are included here, as well as questions about transportation, communication, customs and even grooming both for you and your broomstick. If you know serious skills such as how to detect and avoid your enemies or identify Dark Arts items you'll do just fine. And knowing how to make sure you're on the right end of every Weasleys' Wizard Wheezes product won't hurt either.

In fact, if you've been paying attention, these queries at all levels will seem perfectly plain but if not, they may well cause you some pain. As ever, Dragons are difficult and Phoenixes fair and if you have any sense the Salamanders most certainly won't gray your hair!

THE QUESTIONS

1. What is a Remembrall?

2. How do you catch the Knight Bus?

3. When floo powder is tossed into a fireplace, what color do the flames turn?

4. What phrases are necessary to work the Marauder's Map?

5. What are the times listed on the Weasleys' clock?

6. What are the common household cleaners of the wizarding world?

HINTS!

Remember that wizards don't necessarily have the same sense of time and place as Muggles. Look at the Knight Bus, for example, that travels to destinations based on alphabetical order rather than their proximity to each other. The times on the Weasleys' clock aren't times so much as places.

7. Which Ministry department governs the use of Portkeys?

8. Name the correspondence course on magic targeted at Squibs.

9. As demonstrated by the protection Snape devised for the Sorcerer's (or Philosopher's) Stone, what skill do most wizards lack?

10. Name the magical items known to be available in Borgin and Burkes.

11. At what address does Harry first year school letter finally reach him?

12. How does one access Diagon Alley?

HINTS!

It's actually Hermione who spells this skill wizards lack; who, as the only Muggle-born of the group, also serves to underscore the point. To find this answer consider what qualities Severus Snape and Miss Granger have in common other than bad hair.

13. What candy popular with Muggles is commonly used as a restorative in the wizarding world?

14. What does a Foe-Glass do?

15. What does the Skiving Snackbox do?

16. How old must you be to get your Apparition license?

17. How do you get to Platform 9 ¾?

18. How long is the Ministry sponsored Apparition training course?

HINTS!

It's not just wizards who feel this way about the candy in question. While we may not be battling Dementors, millions of dollars are spent each year studying medical applications of this popular treat.

19. What would the happiest person in the world see in the Mirror of Erised?

20. How does a pensieve work?

21. Who are the famous wandmakers of the wizarding world?

22. In Divination, what does a falcon mean?

23. The flying car that Harry and Ron eventually crash into the Whomping Willow was what model?

24. What is the full and proper name of Filibuster fireworks?

HiNTS!

While American characters are almost entirely absent from the Harry Potter books, this is slightly less true if you consider the flying car in question sentient.

25. What color is the Hogwarts Express?

26. What types of objects are most commonly chosen for Portkeys?

27. What spell would a wizard use instead of a compass?

28. What does Hermione use to get to all her classes in her third year?

29. Where does Narcissa Malfoy prefer to shop?

30. What Diagon Alley store may have inspired the Weasley Twins in their future endeavors?

HINTS!

While she may enjoy the Dark Arts, the answer here is not Borgin and Burkes. Rather you're looking for the name of the dress shop she took her business to after discovering that Madam Malkin catered towards non pure-blood clients.

31. When was Ollivander's founded?

32. What is the name of the ice cream parlor on Diagon Alley?

33. What time does the Hogwarts Express depart?

34. What candies are available on the Hogwarts Trolly?

35. Where does Dumbledore keep his pensieve?

36. How does Harry first become acquainted with the fact that wizarding portraits and photos are not still images like Muggle ones?

HiNTS!

"Where it's easily accessible to Harry" is not, technically, the right answer. But it does seem to be true, doesn't it? And certainly this information should help you find it.

37. What is a Howler?

38. What food is served at Nearly Headless Nick's Deathday Party?

39. What is the more mundane name for a Deluminator?

40. What is a Hand of Glory?

41. What type of quill does Rita Skeeter prefer?

42. Name the contents of a broomstick serving kit.

HINTS!

The Deluminator is one of the very first magical objects we meet in the Harry Potter series, but we don't learn its proper name until nearly the end of the series; a small revelation that seems fitting and familiar in the course of the journey *Harry Potter and the Deathly Hallows* takes us on.

43. How can Muggle photographs be developed to behave like wizarding ones?

44. What would you bring to a wizarding sporting event or concert instead of opera glasses or the like?

45. How does a Sneakascope work?

46. What is the problem with buying a Metamorph Medal?

47. What is the chain of ownership of the flying motorcycle?

48. What Weasley Wheezes candy causes nosebleeds?

HiNTS!

Similar to binoculars both in name and function the device you would bring to a sporting event has many more features.

49. What type of stone was in the cursed necklace Draco tried to use to fulfill his obligation to Voldemort?

50. What is a canary cream?

51. What does a secrecy sensor look like?

52. What commercially available product in the wizarding world is used to repair magical items?

53. What wand statistics are revealed by the device used for the weighing of the wands?

54. Whose mishap with the Vanishing Cabinets gives Draco his idea for using them?

HINTS!

The weighing of the wands may require a magical instrument, but that device tells us nothing that Mr. Ollivander couldn't recite from memory.

55. How many hands does Dumbledore's pocket watch have?

56. What is a probity probe?

57. How would you stop it from raining in someone's office?

58. Other than owls and the floo, how can wizards communicate over distances?

59. Describe the qualities of Goblin-made armor.

60. Describe the products the Weasley Twins aimed at their female audience.

HINTS!

Molly Weasley would certainly be thrilled with Goblin-made armor. Not only would it help keep her family safe, one of its key properties is based on the fact that it never needs cleaning. Why?

61. What was the initial problem with the Fainting Fancy?

62. What do Ministry interdepartmental memos look like?

63. Describe the advertisements at the Quidditch World Cup Harry attended.

64. What is an age line?

65. How did Harry come to possess a wizard chess set?

66. Who drives the Knight Bus?

HINTS!

Had an American written the Harry Potter series, perhaps our hero would have found his chess set as a prize in a Crackerjack box. Harry found his in a festive and similar sounding novelty. What was it?

67. In what card game do the cards explode?

68. It turns out the horses that pull the Hogwarts carriages aren't exactly invisible. What are they?

69. What are the side effects of the Daydream Charm that the Weasley twins sell?

70. From what object is a witch or wizard likely to have heard daily grooming advice?

71. What special abilities does Mad-Eye Moody's eye have?

72. What can a wizard use other than the Sonorus Charm to amplify their voice?

HINTS!

Assume the answer hints at the daily use of something that generally aids in grooming. Chances are Lavender Brown uses one quite a bit; Severus Snape, less so.

73. What is a Dungbomb?

74. Other than the obvious, what does the punching telescope do?

75. Name the one harmless Weasleys' Wizard Wheezes product.

THE ANSWERS!

1. A small ball filled with white smoke, that when touched will turn red if there is something the person touching it has forgotten to do (HP1, chapter 9). While we have no evidence of the Remembrall reminding someone of what that forgotten thing actually is, they are banned from examinations (HP5, chapter 31) and so might be more directly useful than has previously been explained to us.

2. Extend the wand hand (HP3, chapter 3).

3. Green (HP2, chapter 4).

4. "I solemnly swear that I am up to no good" activates the map and "mischief managed" returns it to seemingly ordinary parchment (HP3, chapter 10).

5. As mentioned in the hint, they aren't strictly times, but locations; just as it can be time for school it can be time for hospital or mortal peril. The clock has nine hands, each representing a Weasley, and they can point at any of the

following locations: Home, school, work, traveling, lost, hospital, prison and mortal peril (HP4, chapter 10).

6. Mrs. Scower's Magical Mess Remover (HP2, chapter 9).

7. The Department of Magical Transportation has a Portkey Office (HP5, chapter 7).

8. Kwikspell (HP2, chapter 8). Of course, a true Squib won't be helped by such a thing at all.

9. Logic (HP1, chapter 16). Hermione declares this when she gets a look at Snape's logic puzzle that's designed to guard the Sorcerer's Stone. This should have perhaps been our first clue that Snape was not a pure-blood as was generally assumed until the advent of *Harry Potter and the Half-Blood Prince*.

10. A Hand of Glory, cards stained with blood, a glass eye, some distressing masks, bones, torture instruments, a hangman's rope, an opal necklace and a large black cabinet (HP2, chapter 4). Many of these objects appear again throughout the series with Borgin & Burkes being the indirect source both of many of Harry's problems and many of Draco's bad ideas.

TRIVIA TIDBIT

MAGIC, MYTHS & MUGGLES

The Hand of Glory is a grotesque legend that appears often in works of fantasy and horror. Said to be the pickled left hand (or the hand that committed the crime) of a hanged man, the Hand of Glory when used as a candlestick for a candle with similarly grisly origins (it's made from the fat of the condemned) was said to have powers ranging from ensuring the candle never went out to unlocking doors and freezing people in place. Hands of Glory were actually produced and at least two are on display in museums in England: at the Whitby Museum and the Wasall Museum.

11. "The Floor, Hut-on-the-Rock, The Sea" (HP1, chapter 4).

12. Via Floo or via the courtyard behind The Leaky Cauldron where you have to tap a certain brick three times with your wand for the wall to open (HP1, chapter 5).

13. Chocolate, of course! The most significant example of this appears in *Harry Potter and the Prisoner of Azkaban* when Remus Lupin offers Harry chocolate after an encounter with Dementors.

14. It shows the enemies of its owner (HP4, chapter 20).

15. The Skiving Snackbox is one of the many Weasleys' Wizard Wheezes products designed to help the user avoid the obligations of their choice by producing temporary illnesses. Each candy in the box has two ends – one to produce the illness effect and one to lift it (HP5, chapter 6).

16. You must be seventeen, a legal adult in the wizarding world (HP6, chapter 4).

17. You have to walk through the barrier between platforms 9 and 10. Molly Weasley states that it is important Harry not be scared when he does this, so belief in the ability to pass through to platform 9 ¾ seems to be part of the magic in question (HP1, chapter 6).

18. It is a twelve-week series of lessons with one lesson per week (HP6, chapter 17).

19. Dumbledore says that "the happiest man in the world" would only see himself in the mirror, allowing him to use it as if it weren't magical at all (HP1, chapter 12).

20. A pensieve is essentially a storage device for memories. They can be removed from your head and placed into the basin, thus keeping the mind free of clutter while providing a way to relive them with accuracy or share them with others (HP4, chapter 30).

21. Ollivander is, of course, the most famous and often seen wandmaker (HP1, chapter 5), but in *Harry Potter and the Deathly Hallows* we learn of Gregorovitch who plays an important role in the chain of ownership of the Elder Wand (HP7, chapter 24).

22. The falcon appearing in tea-leaves means that the person who received it has a mortal enemy (HP3, chapter 6).

TRIVIA TIDBIT

MAGIC, MYTH & MUGGLES

Reading tea leaves is a form of tasseography that can also be done with coffee grounds or the residue of wine. The practice originated independently in many countries around the world, including England. It varies to include reading the leaves in plain cups, turning the leaves over onto a dish, or reading the leaves as they fall in specially designed cups with markings on the bottom that indicate the zodiac signs or the dozens of patterns commonly recognized and considered in the practice.

 23. A Ford Angelina (HP2, chapter 3).

 24. Dr. Filibuster's Fabulous No-Heat, Wet-Start Fireworks (HP2, chapter 5).

 25. Scarlet (HP1, chapter 6).

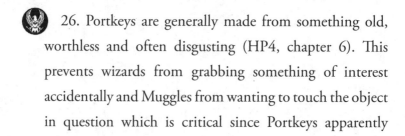 26. Portkeys are generally made from something old, worthless and often disgusting (HP4, chapter 6). This prevents wizards from grabbing something of interest accidentally and Muggles from wanting to touch the object in question which is critical since Portkeys apparently

have the power to transport people regardless of magical ability.

27. The Four Point Spell (HP4, chapter 31). It causes the wand of the witch or wizard who uses it to point north.

28. A Time-Turner (HP3, chapter 21). Although we see Hermione use the device or witness the effects of the device throughout the book we don't learn what it is until Dumbledore instructs her to use it in helping to save Buckbeak.

29. Twilfit & Tatting's (HP6, chapter 6).

TRIVIA TIDBIT

MAGICAL MEANINGS

Tatting is a method for making lace by hand and dates to the early 1800s. Twill, meanwhile is a type of woven fabric with a specific pattern of ribbing. It is suited to warm weather and drapes exceptionally well. Hence the name Twilfit & Tatting easily speaks to Narcissa Malfoy having both expensive and conservative tastes, or, at the very least, exceptional tailoring.

30. Gambol & Japes Joke Shop (HP2, chapter 4).

31. 382 BC (HP1, chapter 5).

32. Florean Fortescue's Ice Cream Parlour (HP3, chapter 4).

33. 11:00 a.m. (HP1, chapter 6).

34. Bertie Bott's Every-Flavor Beans, Droobles Best Blowing Gum, Chocolate Frogs, Pumpkin Pasties, Cauldron Cakes and Liquorice Wands are the named candies. That there are other items is also noted. Also, Harry laments the lack of Mars bars (HP1, chapter 6).

TRIVIA TIDBIT

BRITISH VERSUS AMERICAN

In this case, it's actually British vs. American candy. The British Mars bar is similar to what Americans call a Milky Way. Some American readers may remember a similar candy bar that also contained almonds which was sold in the U.S. until 2000 and is now discontinued.

35. In a cabinet in his office (HP4, chapter 30).

36. When looking at Chocolate frog cards, specifically the one of Dumbledore, while riding on the Hogwarts Express for the first time with Ron (HP1, chapter 6).

37. A Howler is an angry letter whose main and perhaps only purpose is to tell someone off. It arrives smoking, berates the recipient in the loudest tones possible and then explodes (HP2, chapter 6).

38. Fish, cakes, haggis, peanuts and cheese. All the food however was rotten, burnt or otherwise spoilt in some way, which Hermione theorized was to allow the ghosts to taste it. The ghosts can't actually eat, after all, and would just pass through the food. Harry asks one of the ghosts present if he can taste the food when he does this. "Almost," is his sad reply (HP2, chapter 8).

39. A Put-Outer (HP1, chapter 1).

40. In the world of Harry Potter, a Hand of Glory (as described in the Muggle lore discussed earlier in this section) is a shriveled hand which when a candle is placed in it gives light only to the bearer (HP2, chapter 4).

41. Rita Skeeter prefers the Quick-Quotes quill. It doesn't need to be held and seems to transcribe exaggerated and florid accounts of the actual events being discussed (HP4, chapter 18).

42. The one Hermione bought for Harry included *The Handbook of Do-It-Yourself Broomcare*, Fleetwood's High-Finish polish and Tail-Twig clippers (HP3, chapter 1).

43. By using a special developing solution (HP2, chapter 6).

44. Omnioculars. They are like binoculars, but they also have instant replay, slow motion and commentary features, among, possibly, others (HP4, chapter 7).

45. It makes a whistling noise when someone untrustworthy is around (HP3, chapter 1).

46. While they are supposed to give the wearer the abilities of a Metamorphagus, they don't work very well; producing changes the wearer cannot control and sometimes requiring the intervention of St. Mungo's or another healer to reverse (HP6, chapter 5).

47. The motorcycle was originally owned by Sirius Black. Hagrid has it by the time Harry is a baby (HP1, chapter

1) and Arthur is tinkering with it during the war (HP7, chapter 4).

48. Nosebleed Nougat (HP5, chapter 12).

49. Opal (HP6, chapter 12). In fact, this is the opal necklace originally seen in Borgin & Burkes (HP2, chapter 4).

TRIVIA TIDBIT

MAGIC, MYTHS & MUGGLES

The opal has long been the subject of superstition, much of it contradictory. The birthstone for October, it is often considered unlucky to wear for anyone who was not born in that month. In the Middle Ages, however, the opal was considered lucky and it was worn both to protect the eyesight and to help blonde women maintain their hair color. Opals have also been greatly coveted by leaders throughout history, including Mark Antony and Queen Victoria. Currently, most of the world's opals come from Australia.

50. A Weasleys' Wizard Wheezes product that briefly transfigures the person eating this candy into a giant yellow canary (HP4, chapter 21).

51. Old-fashion TV antennas (HP4, chapter 20).

52. Spellotape (HP2, chapter 6).

TRIVIA TIDBIT

BRITISH VS. AMERICAN

What Americans commonly refer to by the brand name Scotch tape is called Sellotape in Britain and is even referenced in chapter two of *Harry Potter and the Philosopher's Stone*.

53. Length, core material, and length of time it's been actively used (HP5, chapter 7).

54. The Weasley twins stuffed Montague into the Vanishing Cabinet (HP5, chapter 17), ultimately giving Draco his idea for how to let the Death Eaters into

Hogwarts.

55. Twelve (HP1, chapter 1).

56. A probity probe detects spells and concealed objects on a wizard. They are used both at the Ministry of Magic (HP5, chapter 7) and Gringotts (HP6, chapter 6) for security.

57. Meteolojinx Recanto (HP7, chapter 13).

58. By using their Patronus as a messenger (HP4, chapter 28).

59. Goblin-made armor is resistant to dirt. It only absorbs that which strengthens it (HP7, chapter 15).

60. The WonderWitch line includes love potions and acne creams (HP6, chapter 6).

61. During testing, the subject, being unconscious, was unable to revive himself without assistance (HP5, chapter 6).

62. Self-directed paper airplanes that zoom throughout the Ministry (HP5, chapter 7).

TRIVIA TIDBIT

MAGIC, MYTHS & MUGGLES

The origin of the paper airplane is a subject of some debate. It is often credited to Leonardo Da Vinci, but there is compelling evidence that they were actually first created as toys by the Chinese approximately 2,000 years ago. The "traditional" paper airplane shape as we know it today is generally credited to Jack Northrop and the version he invented in 1930.

63. It appeared as gold lettering written on a giant blackboard. This blackboard later became the scoreboard once the match began (HP4, chapter 8).

64. When we see it in use it is a line drawn around the Goblet of Fire to prevent anyone under the age of seventeen from approaching it to enter their name into the Goblet (HP4, chapter 12). However, the settings on it are probably variable.

65. He got it in a Christmas cracker (HP1, chapter 12).

66. Ernie Prang drives the Knight Bus (HP3, chapter 3).

67. Exploding Snap (HP2, chapter 15).

68. Thestrals (HP5, chapter 10).

69. A vacant expression and some degree of drooling, presumably only during the thirty minutes the Charm is actually active (HP6, chapter 6).

70. A talking mirror, of course (HP2, chapter 13).

71. It can see through solid objects, behind the user (HP4, chapter 13) and through Invisibility Cloaks (HP4, chapter 19).

72. Magical megaphones are seen in several Quidditch-related contexts (HP2, chapter 14).

73. The wizarding equivalent of a stink bomb. Also, Filch's worst nightmare (HP3, chapter 10).

74. There's a puff of black smoke and a bang to go with that punch (HP6, chapter 5).

75. The one utterly harmless Weasleys' Wizard Wheezes product seems to be pygmy puffs (HP6, chapter 6), which are cute, cuddly pets that squeak and bear an uncanny resemblance to the tribbles of *Star Trek* (without, apparently, eating everything in sight).

QUEST 5

GOVERNMENT, BANKING & BUREAUCRACY

The wizarding world is often excessively detailed without being remotely precise, making it a prime breeding ground for strange laws, complicated regulations and the worst sorts of bureaucracy. But understanding any culture requires knowledge of its legal and banking systems and how they can work both for and against you.

In this Quest we'll be checking your knowledge of everything from the Ministry floor plan to Gringotts vault numbers and the location of key magical communities. Good citizens of the wizarding world will also be expected to know the dates of all sorts of rules, statutes and regulations. Be sure not to restrict your thinking solely to wizarding Britain as the troubles Harry has faced during his battles with Voldemort have had repercussions around the world, and not merely with witches and wizards.

Assuming you're savvy, the Salamander questions should sail right by. Phoenix may require that when it comes to detail, you've had a more careful eye and to rate as a Dragon you'll most certainly have to do more than try.

THE QUESTIONS

1. How many Sickles and Knuts are in a Galleon?

2. What was the number of Sirius Black's vault at Gringotts?

3. When and why did the International Confederation of Wizards establish the right to carry a wand at all times?

4. What title does the head of the Wizengamot hold?

5. How many members does the Wizengamot have?

6. Describe the differences between the concept of ownership amongst Goblins versus wizards.

HINTS!

Carrying a wand at all times was a right established when the wizarding world officially separated and hid from the Muggle one. If you know the date of one event, you know the date of the other; and if you consider the reason for the separation, you have the answer to the other half of this question.

7. What was the name of the student organization under Umbridge that was responsible for helping her uphold the Ministry's educational directives at Hogwarts?

8. Percy Weasley began his Ministry career in what department?

9. What is the name of the Bulgarian Minister of Magic?

10. What vault number at Gringotts held the Sorcerer's (or Philosopher's) stone?

11. Describe the uniforms of the Wizengamot members.

12. What was Bartemus Crouch, Sr.'s chief task with regard to the Quidditch World Cup?

HINTS!

The only time we see the Bulgarian Minister of Magic is at the Quidditch World Cup that Harry attends before the start of his fourth year. This should tell you exactly where to look in *Harry Potter and the Goblet of Fire* for the answer to this question.

13. How does the Ministry govern the use of underage magic?

14. Who employs Hit Wizards?

15. Which Ministry employee contacted Harry about his use of magic outside of Hogwarts?

16. What is contained in the Department of Mysteries?

17. Which Ministry department is the largest?

18. How secure are activities that take place on the Floo Network?

HiNTS!

For the answer to this question concerning use of magic outside of Hogwarts, look on the signature line of the owl Harry receives about his transgression before the start of his fifth year.

19. What is an Unspeakable?

20. What number must you dial in the phone booth at the visitors' entrance to the Ministry of Magic to gain access to the building?

21. Who is Eric Munch?

22. Describe the activities of the Muggle-born Registration Commission.

23. Who was the first Supreme Mugwump of the International Confederation of Wizards?

24. Name the subgroups of the Department of Magical Accidents and Catastrophes.

HINTS!

Eric Munch is a low-level Ministry employee who makes two critical appearances during *Harry Potter and the Order of the Phoenix*. This should show you where to look to find this wizard's job.

25. Where is Azkaban located?

26. What divisions are under the Department of Magical Transportation?

27. Who were the named members of the Inquisitorial Squad?

28. How much does the Ministry of Magic apparition training course cost?

29. Describe the Fountain of Magical Brethren.

30. Who were the Interrogators at Harry's hearing on underage magic use?

HINTS!

During Dolores Umbridge's brief reign as the Headmistress of Hogwarts, Harry Potter and Dumbledore's Army may well have been her number one enemies. Working under the philosophy of "the enemy of my enemy is my friend" which students would then be most likely to sign up for the Inquisitorial Squad?

31. What was the predecessor to the Ministry of Magic?

32. Who was the first person known to escape Azkaban?

33. Describe the curses used as security precautions inside of Gringotts.

34. Which potion with possible uses in a courtroom setting is closely regulated by the Ministry?

35. What prohibits Goblins from using wands?

36. What are Clankers?

HINTS!

Goblins do not, as far as we can see, lack the ability to use wands. Rather, consider how other non-human but sentient creatures are dealt with in the wizarding world. Look at Merpeople, Centaurs and House-elves when considering your answer.

37. What publication did Educational Degree 27 prohibit?

38. Who controls the weather in the Ministry of Magic?

39. Where does one find brains in the Ministry of Magic?

40. Why are flying carpets banned?

41. How are Dragon eggs classified in terms of trade regulations?

42. When was the Werewolf Code of Conduct established?

HiNTS!

While the answer to this Dragon egg question is in *Fantastic Beasts and Where to Find Them*, it may help to remember how Hagrid obtains Norbert in *Harry Potter and the Sorcerer's Stone*.

43. When was the International Statute of Secrecy passed?

44. How do you free a House-elf?

45. Auror Headquarters shares a floor with what other Ministry offices?

46. By what is Gringotts controlled?

47. How did employees enter the Ministry of Magic once it had fallen to the Death Eaters?

48. What were Dolores Umbridge's titles in the Ministry of Magic after the Ministry had fallen to the Death Eaters?

HINTS!

First, you surely already know to look for the answer to question 47 in *Harry Potter and the Deathly Hallows*, because while the Ministry may be incompetent before its fall, it's not actually under Death Eater control until what would have been Harry's final year at Hogwarts; then it and its employees go completely down the drain.

49. What was the slogan of the Ministry under the Death Eater regime?

50. What speed options do the carts that go to the vaults at Gringotts have?

51. Who is known to hold the Order of Merlin, Second Class?

52. Which Goblin helped Harry to his vault the first time he visited Gringotts?

53. How does the Minister of Magic contact the Muggle Prime Minister to warn of an upcoming visit or emergency that needs to be discussed?

54. To what four events in the wizarding world has the Muggle Prime Minister been alerted?

Hints!

Hogwarts headmasters turn to these magical items for advice and Hermione even attempts to use one to spy on Snape. Name the item and you've found the method.

55. If Sirius had not explicitly left Harry Grimmauld Place, to whom would it have gone?

56. What was the Ministry searching for during the raid at Malfoy Manor?

57. Once the International Statute of Secrecy was enacted, what towns became havens for witches and wizards and developed strong magical communities?

58. What position did Dirk Cresswell hold at the Ministry?

59. In which division of the Department for the Regulation and Control of Magical Creatures did Newt Scamander work?

60. Which parts of wizarding law was Harry accused of violating at his hearing before the start of his fifth year?

HINTS!

Cresswell's actions during the war might help you figure out what his job was before everything in the wizarding world went pear-shaped. The Muggle-born Registration Commission tried to send him to Azkaban, but he escaped, living as a fugitive with Dean Thomas and two creatures of another magical species. Name the species, and you can easily find Cresswell's job from there.

61. Kingsley Shacklebolt worked with Muggles in what capacity?

62. Which clause of the wand-use code prevents use by non-human creatures?

63. According to Percy Weasley, Vampires are addressed under which set of Ministry regulations?

64. Which piece of legislation did Arthur Weasley help write?

65. Which Educational Decree made Filch enjoy his job much more?

66. Venomous Tentacula seeds are which class of non-tradable substance?

HiNTS!

No matter how crazy life at the Ministry can be, never forget that Arthur Weasley loves his job because it involves working with the subjects that fascinate him. If you consider Arthur's obsessions you'll quickly find the answer to this question.

67. Which Ministry liaison office has never been used?

68. Name the one *Obliviator* whose name we know.

69. How large was Arthur Weasley's staff when he was working for the Office for the Detection and Confiscation of Counterfeit Defensive Spells and Protective Objects?

70. Who works in the Misuse of Muggle Artifacts Office with Arthur Weasley?

71. Which witch works in the Ministry's Floo Regulation department?

72. Various spies were active throughout the wizarding world during the two wars with Voldemort. What was the name of the Dark Lord's spy within the Ministry of Magic?

HINTS!

If you can't get the answer to question 69 one way, try it another: Mr. Weasley's staff is approximately one-fifth the size of the Wizengamot.

73. Who works on the Committee on Experimental Charms?

74. Who did Percy try to persuade to sign the International Ban on Dueling?

75. Name the three Ministry offices that address Werewolf issues.

THE ANSWERS!

1. A Galleon is worth 17 Sickles and since there are 29 Knuts in a Sickle there are 493 Knuts in a Galleon (HP1, chapter 5).

2. 711 (HP3, chapter 22).

3. The right to carry a wand at all times was determined in 1692 by the International Confederation of Wizards. This was at the peak of hostilities between Muggles and wizards and as the wizarding world was in the midst of separating and shielding itself from the Muggle one (Q).

TRIVIA TIDBIT

HISTORY: MUGGLE & MAGICAL

The Salem witch trials in the Massachusetts Bay Colony were in 1692. Twenty people were executed as part of the witch hunt that began when the unusual behavior of two young girls was attributed to the Devil. The trials continued into the following year, but none of the accused was found guilty in 1693.

TRIVIA TIDBIT

...CONTINUED

The Salem accused and convicted in order of their 1692 executions were: Bridget Bishop, Sarah Wildes, Elizabeth Howe, Susannah Martin, Sarah Good, Rebecca Nurse, George Burroughs, Martha Carrier, George Jacobs, John Proctor, John Willard, Giles Corey, Martha Corey, Mary Easty, Alice Parker, Mary Parker, Ann Pudeator, Wilmott Redd, Margaret Scott and Samuel Wardwell. Contrary to popular belief none of the accused was burned at the stake; with one exception that died from torture, they were all hanged. There is no reason today to believe that any of them were witches or wizards or guilty of the crimes of which they were accused. Considering how little of the Americas we see in the Harry Potter series, you may be surprised to see this reference to events in the so-called New World. However, it is important to remember that in 1692 the Massachusetts Bay Colony was a British possession.

4. Chief Warlock. We first see this title used for Dumbledore in chapter 4 of *Harry Potter and the Sorcerer's Stone*, but at that point we do not know over what body the Chief Warlock reigns, if any. It is only later as we learn about the Ministry's structure in *Harry Potter and the Order of the Phoenix* and when Dumbledore temporarily loses this and a number of other positions, that this structure is entirely clear.

TRIVIA TIDBIT

MAGIC, MYTH & MUGGLES

The etymology of the word "warlock" is generally accepted to be from an Old English word meaning "oath breaker." As such, this is a fascinating title both in terms of its use as regards the leader of the Wizengamot and as regards Dumbledore's own history. Because the Ministry is portrayed alternately as foolish or malicious, it is not surprising, considering J. K. Rowling's sense of humor throughout the series that a word with this type of negative connotation would come into play about a senior Ministry position. The origins of the title are perhaps even more fascinating when applied to Dumbledore directly, considering the various betrayals we ultimately learn he committed over the course of his life, largely to do what he believed was right and necessary to save the wizarding world not just from Voldemort but its own worst proclivities. This meaning of a protector, despite seeming contradictory, is also deeply embedded in the word. *The Oxford English Dictionary* cites an archaic form of "warlock" that places it as a verb meaning "to bar against hostile invasion," which is certainly one of the many tasks Dumbledore performed throughout his life.

5. Approximately five (HP5, chapter 8).

6. As far as Goblins are concerned the being that creates an object has ultimate rights over it, even above that of the purchaser. When a Goblin-made object is sold they essentially consider it leased to the one who paid for it. Wizards and witches pass down Goblin-made property in inheritances which is highly problematic for Goblins as they believe the objects should be returned to their Goblin roots upon the death of the original purchaser. This not happening is essentially viewed by Goblins as stealing (HP7, chapter 25).

7. The Inquisitorial Squad (HP5, chapter 7).

8. Percy's first job was in the Department for International Cooperation (HP4, chapter 5).

9. We only learn his last name which may be either Oblansk or Obalonsk (HP4, chapter 8). Or something entirely different all together since Cornelius Fudge can't seem to manage it correctly.

10. 713 (HP1, chapter 5).

11. Wizengamot members wear plum-colored robes. On the left side of the chest they have an ornate silver W insignia (HP5, chapter 8).

12. From his complaints in chapter seven of *Harry Potter and the Goblet of Fire* it seems clear that arranging Portkeys from around the world was just one of the many taxing annoyances he dealt with, but the only specific one clearly and directly related to the Quidditch World Cup.

13. Underage wizards are not permitted to do magic outside of Hogwarts. This is governed by the Decree for the Reasonable Restriction of Underage Sorcery (HP5, chapter 8).

14. The Ministry of Magic (HP3, chapter 10). These seem to be the equivalent of a police force or FBI-like responsibility, as their job seems to be to pursue criminals (as opposed to the specific focus of Aurors on Dark Wizards).

15. Mafalda Hopkirk (HP5, chapter 2).

16. The central area of the Department of Mysteries is a circular room with twelve handleless doors that rotate around the room at great speed when they are all closed. Only some of what lies behind the twelve doors is known. The Hall of Prophecies is accessed through the Time Room (HP5, chapter 34).

17. The Department of Magical Law Enforcement (FB).

18. Not very. The Floo Network can be monitored both for traffic across it and conversations conducted on it. If there are any regulations restricting the Floo Network Authority's ability to do this, it is unknown (HP5, chapter 7).

19. Unspeakables are Ministry employees who work in the Department of Mysteries. What any one of them does is largely unknown (HP4, chapter 7).

20. 6-2-4-4-2 (HP5, chapter 7), which happens to spell MAGIC on a standard telephone dial.

21. He is a watchwizard repeatedly seen on duty at the Ministry of Magic (HP5, chapter 7). He is also the person who apprehended Sturgis Podmore loitering outside the Department of Mysteries (HP5, chapter 14).

22. According to the Daily Prophet the commission was investigating how Muggle-borns had come to possess magical knowledge. According to the Ministry under Death Eater control, magic can only be inherited from wizarding ancestry. Of course, readers know this to not be true, but it is this world view that informed the Muggle-born Registration Commissions task of identifying, interrogating and incarcerating Muggle-borns for "stealing" magic (HP7, chapter 11).

23. Pierre Bonaccord (HP5, chapter 31).

24. The subgroups include the Accidental Magic Reversal Squad, Obliviator Headquarters and the Muggle-Worthy Excuse Committee (HP5, chapter 7).

25. In the North Sea (HP3, chapter 3).

26. The known divisions are the Floo Network Authority, Broom Regulatory Control, the Portkey Office and the Apparition Test Center (HP5, chapter 7).

27. Draco Malfoy, Vincent Crabbe, Gregory Goyle, Pansy Parkinson, Millicent Bulstrode, Warrington and Montague (HP5, chapter 28).

28. Twelve Galleons (HP6, chapter 17).

29. The fountain shows a wizard and grouped around him a witch, a Centaur, a House-elf and a Goblin. The non-human Beings are apparently gazing up adoringly at the humans (HP5, chapter 7). While this statue is far more benign than what replaces it in the Ministry under the Death Eaters it still shows the biases of the wizarding world.

Trivia Tidbit

Magic, Myth & Muggles

Of all the magical creatures J. K. Rowling uses in her books, the Goblins are perhaps the most problematic to find the Muggle mythological origins of; simply because they have so many. Goblins have a wide range of physical and personality attributes across many cultures; with the only unifying theme being that they are generally unpleasant. The matter up for debate is usually just *how* unpleasant. Are they merely nuisances or actually dangerous? The wizarding world seems to share this ambivalence on Goblins; refusing to give them equal rights (they cannot carry wands) and not compromising with them on Goblin-made objects ownership issues. At the same time, the Goblins have a financial monopoly that probably supplies them with a great deal of power in wizarding politics. While we never see the dwellings of J. K. Rowling's Goblins, in myth they usually live outdoors in the clefts made by rock formations or tree roots.

30. Cornelius Fudge, Amelia Bones and Dolores Umbridge (HP5, chapter 8).

31. The Wizards' Council (FB).

32. Barty Crouch, Jr. (HP4, chapter 27).

33. Gemino and Flagrante Curses (HP7, chapter 26)

34. Veritaserum (HP4, chapter 27).

35. Dated Goblin rebellions have taken place in the 1600s (HP1, chapter 5) and 1700s (HP4, chapter 15) and continue to be an issue.

36. Clankers are the metal devices the Gringotts Goblins use to control the Dragons that guard some of the more well-protected vaults. The Dragons, which are blind, have been trained to back away from the sound these magical metal rattles make (HP7, chapter 26).

37. The Quibbler (HP5, chapter 26).

38. Magical Maintenance (HP7, chapter 12).

39. This is not actually a trick question. The brains are found in tanks behind one of the doors off the circular rooms in the Department of Mysteries. Luna thought they were Aquavirius maggots (HP5, chapter 34).

40. The Registry of Proscribed Charmable Artifacts lists carpets as Muggle Artifacts. For this reason they cannot be charmed into flying carpets nor can flying carpets be imported into the country (HP4, chapter 7).

41. They are Class A Non-Tradable Goods (FB).

42. 1637 (HP1, chapter 16).

TRIVIA TIDBIT

HISTORY: MUGGLE & MAGICAL

Other notable events in 1637 (other than the establishment of the Werewolf Code of Conduct) include Pierre de Fermat writing what would become known as his last theorem, the collapse of the tulip speculation bubble in what is now known as the Netherlands, and the founding of the first town (Tauton, MA) in America by a woman (Elizabeth Poole).

---

43. 1692 (FB).

44. House-elves (which generally dress in placemats, tea cozies and other non-clothing items) are freed by the gift of clothes from their owner. Even an accidental gift,

such as the sock Harry tricks Lucius Malfoy into giving to Dobby, is effective (HP2, chapter 18). By and large, though, these creatures prefer servitude and would find such a gift shameful. Dobby, who dies a proud, free elf is, of course, the most notable exception to this rule.

45. Improper Use of Magic, The Misuse of Muggle Artifacts and Wizengamot Administration Services (HP5, chapter 7).

46. Goblins (HP1, chapter 5), until the Ministry falls to the Death Eaters, at which point it is noted that their control is no longer absolute (HP7, chapter 15).

47. By flushing themselves into the Ministry via charmed public toilets that serve as the employees' entrance (HP7, chapter 12).

48. Senior Undersecretary to the Minister and Head of the Muggle-born Registration Commission (HP7, chapter 13).

49. Magic is Might (HP7, chapter 12).

50. The Gringotts carts have only one speed and it's faster than Hagrid or, we can assume any patron, finds comfortable (HP1, chapter 5).

51. Newton Artemis Fido Scamander (FB).

52. Griphook was the named goblin. There was also an unnamed goblin that directed Harry and Hagrid to Griphook when they first entered and presented their business (HP1, chapter 5).

53. Via magical portrait (HP6, chapter 1), demonstrating that these sentient portraits are not restricted to the dead or imaginary, as often seems to be the case.

54. The escape of Sirius Black from Azkaban, the anti-Muggle actions of Death Eaters at the Quidditch World Cup (and some magical creature importations on the side), the escape of multiple Death Eaters from Azkaban and the murders, curses and other acts of destruction that herald the start of the wizarding war that culminates in *Harry Potter and the Deathly Hallows* (HP6, chapter 1).

55. Bellatrix Black (HP3, chapter 6), his cousin and closest living relative.

56. They were searching for Dark Arts materials and artifacts that were presumably illegal.

57. Godric's Hollow, Tinworth, Upper Flagley and

Ottery St. Catchpole (HP7, chapter 16).

58. Head of the Goblin Liaison Office (HP6, chapter 4).

59. The Beast Division (FB)

60. Harry was accused of violating Paragraph C of the previously mentioned Decree for the Reasonable Restriction of Underage Sorcery and of violating section thirteen of the Statute of Secrecy (HP5, chapter 8). It seems clear that he had committed at least two offenses – doing magic outside of Hogwarts and doing it in front of a Muggle.

61. Shacklebolt was assigned to work with the Muggle Prime Minister, posing as his secretary (HP6, chapter 1).

62. Clause 3 (HP4, chapter 9).

63. *Guidelines for the Treatment of Non-Wizard Part-Humans* (HP4, chapter 10).

64. The Muggle Protection Act (HP2, chapter 4).

65. Number 29. We don't know what it says precisely,

but he noted how he'd like to string up Harry in his office, and that when this decree came through he would be allowed to (HP5, chapter 28).

 66. Class C (HP5, chapter 9).

 67. The Centaur Liaison Office (FB).

TRIVIA TIDBIT

MAGIC, MYTH & MUGGLES

In Greek mythology Centaurs are a race of half-horse, half-human creatures that may have come into mythology as a reaction to a non-horse riding society encountering mounted warriors for the first time. In myth, the Centaurs were said to inhabit the mountains of Thessaly. Perhaps not surprisingly, the Thessalian tribes described by the ancient Greeks were the inventors of horseback riding.

---

 68. Arnold Peasegood (HP4, chapter 7).

 69. Ten people (HP6, chapter 5).

70. Perkins (HP2, chapter 3).

71. Madam Edgecomb (HP5, chapter 27).

72. Augustus Rookwood (HP4, chapter 30).

73. Gilbert Whimple (HP4, chapter 7).

74. The Transylvanians (HP4, chapter 23).

75. Werewolf Support Services, Werewolf Registry and Werewolf Capture Unit (FB).

QUEST 6

SPORTS, ENTERTAINMENT & LEISURE

What would the point of magic be if you couldn't have fun with it? Certainly, it seems unlikely that any witch or wizard has ever tried to answer such a question. After all, even Severus Snape seemed to take an interest in Quidditch, and Argus Filch, an infamous squib, certainly finds delight in the prospect of punishing miscreants.

Yes, the magical world offers fun for everyone whether you enjoy the song stylings of Celestina Warbeck or prefer the grisly delights of Troll hunting. Above all, though, fun in the magical world is often about sport; which is why you'll find most, but not all, of the questions below to be related to the wonderful world of Quidditch. Before you get too confident, remember that those desiring a Dragon rating ought to know about dueling, while Phoenix will surely require some knowledge beyond your ordinary schooling; even Salamanders might find this test grueling!

THE QUESTIONS

1. Who wrote *Quidditch Through the Ages*?

2. When and why did the Quaffle become scarlet?

3. Name the members of the Bulgarian National Team at the Quidditch World Cup.

4. Where is the Museum of Quidditch located?

5. According to Dumbledore's intro to the Muggle edition of *Quidditch Though the Ages*, in what emotion are wizards and witches who support the Chudley Cannons united?

6. The Wizard's Council issued three rulings regarding how far from Muggles Quidditch matches could be played. Name the years and distances involved.

HINTS!

Quidditch Through the Ages was one of two books Rowling published to raise money for Comic Relief U. K. The other book she released to benefit this cause was *Fantastic Beasts and Where to Find Them*.

7. Why were broomsticks chosen as the objects wizards use to fly?

8. When did flying broomsticks first appear in the European wizarding world?

9. The annual broom race in Sweden covers the distance between which two cities?

10. Why were the original Quidditch baskets replaced with goal posts?

11. When was *The Noble Sport of Warlocks* written?

12. When did the Quaffle become enchanted?

HINTS!

While wizards may be bad at logic, they often do things for perfectly sensible reasons. One example is the replacement of the baskets originally used in Quidditch with uniform goal posts that's asked about in question ten. Even if you don't know much about the wizarding world's favorite sport, there's a word in this hint that should help anyone guess this Salamander answer.

13. Why is Quidditch not particularly popular in Asia?

 14. Throughout the history of Quidditch, Bludgers have been made out of different materials at different times. Describe this evolution of materials.

 15. Name a song by Celestina Warbeck.

 16. To what would you have to tune in to hear The Weird Sisters on the radio?

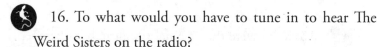 17. Describe the demise of the Banchory Bangers.

18. How much does a copy of *Quidditch Through the Ages* cost?

HINTS!

Can't remember much about Celestina Warback? Don't worry, a lot of people can't stand her music. Molly Weasley, however, is a huge fan, especially around the holiday season, which should help you solve definitely difficult question 15.

MAGICAL MUSIC BY MUGGLES

Increasingly, Muggles have been inspired to make music about the wizarding world. There are, at present, dozens of these "wizard rock" or "wrock" bands, some of which tour nationally and internationally performing at small clubs, libraries and Harry Potter conferences and other special events. Many of the bands are named after Harry Potter characters and sometimes take on the personas of the characters in question for performance purposes.

Notable wizard rock bands include Harry and the Potters, Draco and the Malfoys and The Remus Lupins. Also out there are The Sectumsempras, The Hermione Crookshanks Experience, The Hungarian Horntails (who served as the horn section for a recent Harry and the Potters gig in New York City), Oliver Boyd and the Remembralls, and The Parselmouths. Wizard rock is becoming so popular with fans of all ages that events focusing entirely on wizard rock, such as October 2007's Wrockstock in Missouri, are increasingly cropping up.

19. Which Ministry department regulates Quidditch in wizarding Britain?

20. Describe the two wizarding games that feature the bladders of Beasts.

21. What was the original term for a Quidditch referee?

22. From whom did Harry get his first broom?

23. How did the spectators participate in early Quidditch?

24. In what year and with what final change did the Quidditch Pitch cease to alter?

HINTS!

Question 23 is another Quidditch query you can probably puzzle out with a bit of help. Consider the origins of Quidditch and the use of the Golden Snidget. How was it kept within the bounds of the Pitch? Answer that and add another Phoenix feather to your cap.

GAMES MUGGLES PLAY

Muggles, having learned of Quidditch through the Harry Potter books, have created multiple versions of the sport suitable for those without access to magic. Rules vary as the sport remains too new to have been standardized in the same way that true, wizarding Quidditch has. Muggles often adopt tools from other sports for their games of Quidditch, using soccer fields as Pitches, and soccer or basketballs as Quaffles. Sometimes a Frisbee, despite its entirely incorrect shape, will be used as a Quaffle for its better aerodynamic properties. Bludgers, when used, are generally something soft; some rule sets merely allow for the Beaters to tackle players as in Rugby or American Football. Brooms are occasionally used, but not to any great effect. Players generally run about on their own two legs, but versions of the game involving skateboards, scooters and even bicycles also exist. The biggest problem for Muggle Quidditch, of course, is the Snitch. There is simply no comparable object available and most rule sets involve "Snitch substitutes," usually in the form of one or more people. In some versions, the Snitch is a single person allowed to roam a ridiculously large area; or multiple "Snitch substitutes" are released onto the field, all carrying Snitches, but only one is actually golden. Quidditch is often played on college campuses, or one can participate in one of the Quidditch tournaments or pick-up matches played at the Harry Potter academic and fan conferences that take place all over the world.

25. What is the Golden Snidget?

26. Where is a feral Snitch rumored to reside?

27. In Aingingein what was the Dom?

28. Which is the most successful team of the British and Irish League?

29. What is the purpose of the Sloth Grip Roll?

30. What was the most dangerous game involving brooms and when was it outlawed?

HINTS!

If you can figure out what a sloth grip looks like, you can figure out what a Sloth Grip Roll is for. Aside from doing some research on the rather non-magical tree-dwelling sloth you may want to check out some of the Harry Potter films with Hogwarts Quidditch matches. There you can see the roll in action!

31. Where did Quidditch originate?

32. How did the point value of the Golden Snitch come to be?

33. Which Hogwarts professor was a dueling champion?

34. In Quidditch what was the original name of the Bludger?

35. Describe the appropriate formalities that must be observed for commencing a duel.

36. Who invented the Golden Snitch?

HINTS!

Kenneth Branagh as Gilderoy Lockhart shows off dueling formalities and the answer to this question in the film of *Harry Potter and the Chamber of Secrets.*

37. What was the final score at the Quidditch World Cup match Harry attended before the start of his fourth year?

38. In wizarding Britain what are the requirements for Quidditch referees?

39. In what year was the first complete description of Quidditch written?

40. For which Quidditch position is gender most likely a concern?

41. How many types of Quidditch fouls exist?

42. When was the first Quidditch World Cup?

Hints!

Remember, wizards are creative. That means there are a lot of fouls in Quidditch. To help you on your way, the amount has three digits, but none of those numbers are three.

43. Why is the Twigger 90 looked down upon?

44. When was the ban on the use of wands against the opposing team in Quidditch enacted?

45. When was a limit established on the number of teams to compete for the England and Ireland Quidditch League Cup?

46. In dueling, what is a second?

47. What famous Quidditch player is the mother of the lead guitarist for The Weird Sisters?

48. What are the ten most common fouls in Quidditch?

HiNTS!

The limit on the number of professional teams that compete for the Cup was established in the same year as the League itself. If you know one date, you know the other.

49. How often is the Quidditch World Cup held?

50. Name the teams that compete in the England and Ireland Quidditch League Cup.

51. Which 15th century French wizard included Quidditch in a play?

52. Why are the Holyhead Harpies unique?

53. What is the current motto of the Chudley Cannons?

54. Who is the Chairwizard of the International Association of Quidditch?

HINTS!

Most Quidditch Beaters are wizards. Not so with the Holyhead Harpies, and that should tell you enough to remember what makes their team special.

55. Name the mascot of the Ballycastle Bats who is particularly famous for his appearance in butterbeer advertisements.

56. Which Quidditch team is particularly a family enterprise?

57. Describe what use of wands is permissible on the Quidditch Pitch.

58. What caused Harry to crash so badly during a Quidditch game that his broom was destroyed?

59. What happened to the most famous player on the Caerphilly Catapults?

60. What is the first rule in *The Beaters' Bible*?

HINTS!

Have you ever seen someone use a wand on the Quidditch Pitch? But don't be too hasty in declaring that the answer is "none." They are allowed, so there must be a reason.

61. Name the first broom designed for sporting use.

62. The Quidditch Pitch has boundaries in how many dimensions?

63. What is a Bludger backbeat?

64. How did Harry catch his first Snitch?

65. Name the Seeker for the Fitchburg Finches.

66. What African countries have strong Quidditch teams?

HINTS!

This Quidditch technique is practically given away by its name. And you've seen it used in the Hogwarts matches of the Harry Potter films.

67. Why is the New Zealand Ministry of Magic so concerned with Maori art?

68. Why are the Winbourne Wasps so named?

69. Name the most well known European Quidditch teams.

70. Who was Stubby Boardman?

71. What is Quodpot?

72. What game is Nearly-Headless Nick unable to play due to his nearly-headless status?

73. How many people did the stadium built for the Quidditch World Cup Harry attended before the start of his fourth year seat?

74. How does wizard chess differ from Muggle chess?

75. How often was the Triwizard Tournament held before it was discontinued due to an excessive number of casualties?

THE ANSWERS!

1. Kennilworthy Whisp (Q).

2. The Quaffle became scarlet in 1711. The color change occurred after the realization that a naturally colored Quaffle was incredibly hard to find when it hit the ground on a muddy Pitch (Q).

3. Ivanova, Zograf, Levski, Volchanov, Volkov and, of course, Viktor Krum (HP4, chapter 8).

4. London (Q).

5. Despair (Q).

6. In 1362 the Wizards' Council banned Quidditch within fifty miles of towns. Then in 1368 the illegal play area was expanded to a one hundred mile zone. Finally, in 1419, in a clear fit of exasperation, the Council banned the playing of Quidditch anywhere at all where there was any chance at all of a Muggle seeing it. Threatened punishment for violating this decree involved being chained to a dungeon wall. Zacharias Mumps' statement on this matter in 1398

is not relevant to this question as he was not affiliated with the Wizards' Council in any fashion (Q).

7. Broomsticks met the basic requirements wizards and witches felt were important for a flying object: they were inexpensive, easy to carry and aroused no curiosity from Muggles. Broomsticks, of course, are not the only method of magical object transportation used by wizards, and carpets are preferred in the East (Q).

8. The use of broomsticks for flying in Europe is currently dated to 962 CE (Q).

9. Sweden's annual broom race requires fliers to travel from Kopparberg to Arjeplog (Q).

10. Baskets were not standardized in size and caused inequities on the Pitch. In 1883 the Department of Magical Games and Sports mandated hoops of a regulation size (Q).

11. 1620 (Q).

12. The Quaffle became enchanted in 1875 with the advent of Gripping Charms, making the previous century's color change of the ball less relevant (Q).

13. Because broom transportation is less common in Asia there is less interest in the sport. Additionally the ministries of the most prominent carpet producing countries have a somewhat negative view of the sport. Japan, however, is an exception to this rule, and the sport has been gaining ground there (Q).

14. The original Bludgers were made from rock, but because these rocks could be reduced to flying gravel in the course of a game, metal became a better choice of material. The first metal Bludgers were made of lead, but since that metal was too soft to prevent dents that affected their flying ability, Bludgers were eventually switched to iron which remains today as the material of choice (Q).

15. "You Charmed the Heart Right Out of Me" and "A Cauldron Full of Hot Strong Love" are the two Celestina Warbeck song titles we know of thanks to Molly Weasley's enthusiasm for her (HP6, chapter 16). Warbeck also recorded the team anthem for Puddlemere United (Q).

16. The Wizarding Wireless Network (HP4, chapter 22).

17. The Banchory Bangers were disbanded by the Ministry in 1814 because of their extreme disregard for Ministry regulations about secrecy. The team allowed

their Bludgers to escape after a match and then went out, apparently without the aid of any concealment charms, to capture a mascot – a Dragon – for their team (Q).

18. 14 Sickles, 3 Knuts (Q).

19. The Department of Magical Games and Sports (Q).

20. Swivenhodge and Stichstock both use inflated animal bladders – that of pigs and Dragons respectively. While Stickstock hasn't been played for centuries, Swivenhodge still has a small following (Q).

21. Quijudge (Q).

22. Professor McGonogall (HP1, chapter 10).

23. When Quidditch was still being played with the Golden Snidget, spectators participated in the game by casting repelling spells at the Snidget in order to keep it within bounds on the Pitch (Q).

24. The 1883 switch from baskets to hoops was the last change the modern Quidditch Pitch has seen (Q).

25. The Golden Snidget is a gravely endangered bird

that was a popular target of sport hunting and became the predecessor of the Golden Snitch. Prior to the introduction of the Snidget there was no Seeker in Quidditch and it was a game of basic goal scoring (Q).

26. A feral Snitch may reside near Bodmin Moor due to an 1884 match where it eluded capture for six months and both teams eventually abandoned it and the game with it. Some of those residing in the area claim the thing is still living in the area (Q).

27. The Dom was the name of the ball in the game of Aingingein. Generally it was actually a goat gallbladder. (Q).

28. The Montrose Magpies. They've won the league thirty-two times (Q).

29. The Sloth Grip Roll (which looks exactly like it sounds – you hang from the broom like a sloth while rolling) is a technique for avoiding Bludgers (Q).

30. Creaothceann was the most dangerous broom game, but the problem wasn't the brooms. The problem was that the point of the game was essentially to be hit on the head by rocks (Q).

31. Queerditch Marsh (Q).

32. Baberus Bragge, Chief of the Wizards' Council, brought a Golden Snidget to a Quidditch match in 1269 and offered the one who caught it 150 Galleons. Subsequently, once the Snidget (later replaced by the Snitch to protect the endangered birds) was made a formal part of Quidditch the assigned point value was 150 in memory of this frankly exorbitant stunt (150 Galleons then would be over one million Galleons in today's money) (Q).

33. Professor Flitwick (HP2, chapter 11).

34. The Blooder. Aptly named, eh? (Q).

35. We don't ever get a good, clean look at the dueling formalities because of the people involved in the duels that we see. The most useful in this regard is the formal demonstration duel between Snape and Lockhart in which we see them face each other and bow before taking their positions on the area marked out for competition (HP2, chapter 11). That said, Lockhart is mainly interested in showing off and Snape is mainly interested in showing his contempt, so how good a model for dueling manners these two men are is somewhat debatable.

TRIVIA TIDBIT

BOOK VERSUS MOVIE

The film of *Harry Potter and the Chamber of Secrets* gives us somewhat more to go on in terms of the formalities of magical dueling. We see that Snape and Lockhart are competing on a strip essentially like the piste used in fencing, although it is raised and appears to be longer. Additionally, they not only bow, but also salute each other with their wands before taking a garde position like the one alluded to in chapter eleven. There they are described as holding their wands in a manner similar to swords. In the film we even see them use their non-wand hand for balance, similar, but not identical to the use of the off hand for balance in Muggle fencing.

 36. Bowman Wright (Q).

 37. 160 for Bulgaria to 170 for Ireland (HP4, chapter 8).

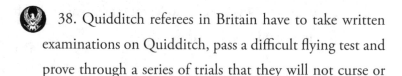 38. Quidditch referees in Britain have to take written examinations on Quidditch, pass a difficult flying test and prove through a series of trials that they will not curse or

otherwise harm problematic players (Q). All of which has to make you wonder why on earth anyone thought Snape refereeing a game, even a school-level one, was remotely a good idea (HP2).

39. 1398 (Q).

40. While witches and wizards generally compete side-by-side and against each other in Quidditch, men usually take the position of Beater because of the physical strength required to effectively knock a Bludger to the other side of the Pitch (Q).

41. Seven hundred are documented, although the Ministry will not release the complete list lest anyone use it for inspiration. Most of these are easily preventable as long as players don't use wands against the other team (Q).

42. 1473 (Q). This, however, is a problematic date. Harry attended the Quidditch World Cup in 1994, which is exactly 521 years after 1473. Five hundred twenty-one is absolutely, positively, one of those numbers not evenly divisible by four, meaning that if each Quidditch World Cup was held in its appropriate year the 130th Quidditch World Cup would have taken place in 1993, leaving Harry with little to see and the Death Eaters with little

to terrorize in 1994. Of course, there may well have been an interruption in the regularity of the Quidditch World Cup, but that is not currently documented. Additionally, wizards are notoriously bad at logic (HP1, chapter 16), and, therefore, one would also have to assume math, meaning, of course, that someone might just have counted wrong one year. Certainly, however, this and the fact that Ludo Bagman declares the 1994 World Cup to be the 422nd such competition (HP4, chapter 8), does present wizard and Muggle readers alike with a significant conundrum.

43. The Twigger was designed to be the best broom on the market, overtaking the dominance of the Nimbus line, but it has structural problems at high speeds and has several features deemed to be silly or unnecessary, giving it a poor reputation among serious players (Q).

44. 1750 (Q).

45. The number of professional teams was limited to thirteen in 1674 when the Britain and Ireland League was established. The main reason for this was the ongoing need for secrecy of the sport (Q).

46. The second takes over the matter of the challenge in case of the death of the primary participant in the duel (HP1, chapter 9).

TRIVIA TIDBIT

GAMES MUGGLES PLAY

In the Muggle version of dueling, which occurred historically in Western countries with both swords and pistols for centuries, the second was also a trusted representative who was the duelist's advocate – he helped arrange the field of challenge and also checked the weapons to make sure the contest was fair. Each participant in the duel had his own second (sometimes more than one, depending on the custom of time and place). The second was also the one who would serve as a witness to the proceedings and convey the news of a loss to interested parties should the duel have resulted in death.

47. Catriona McCormack is Kirley's mother. Her daughter, Meaghan also plays for the team she led to League victory twice in the 1960s, Pride of Portree.

48. Blagging (grabbing an opponent's broom), Blatching (attempting to collide with opponent), Blurting (crossing brooms with an opponent to control their steering), Bumphing (hitting Bludgers towards spectators to stop game action), Cobbing (elbowing), Flacking (blocking

shots from behind the goal hoop instead of from in front of it), Haversacking (placing the Quaffle through the goal hoop instead of throwing it), Quaffle-pocking (damaging the Quaffle to affect its movements), Snitchnip (non-Seekers interacting with the Snitch), Stooging (multiple chasers in the scoring area) (Q).

 49. Every four years.

TRIVIA TIDBIT

GAMES MUGGLES PLAY

While the game-play of Quidditch may be more analogous to that of Cricket, the nearly world-wide enthusiasm the game receives mirrors that of soccer (or football for European readers). The World Cup in soccer is the most famous international competition in the sport and the one fans most seek to flock too. Like the Quidditch World Cup, it is held every four years.

---

50. The Appleby Arrows, the Ballycastle Bats, the Caerphilly Catapults, the Chudley Cannons, the Falmouth Falcons, the Holyhead Harpies, the Kenmare Kestrels, the Montrose Magpies, the Pride of Portree, Puddlemere

United, the Tutshill Tornados, the Wigtown Wanderers and the Wimbourne Wasps (Q).

51. Malecrit (Q).

52. They are the only professional Quidditch team that has always been all female (Q).

TRIVIA TIDBIT

MAGIC, MYTH & MUGGLES

Harpies in mythology were bird-women who were often seen as supernatural creatures representing death and punishment. In the ancient Greek story of Phineas, Zeus punished the king by placing him on an island with an endless buffet of food he could never eat, in part, because the Harpies constantly stole the morsels he was about to place in his mouth. It was Jason and the Argonauts that finally drove the Harpies away and ended Phineas' punishment.

53. "Let's all just keep our fingers crossed and hope for the best." It used to be the much more positive "We shall conquer," but that has recently looked unlikely (Q).

54. Hassan Mostafa (HP4, chapter 8).

55. A fruit bat named Barny who happens to be featured in Butterbeer advertisements (Q).

56. The Wigtown Wanderers were founded by seven siblings. Additionally, descendents of the founding family (the Parkins) have often played on the team (Q).

57. The rules of Quidditch only stipulate what use of wands is not permitted, not what use is. We know wands are allowed on the Pitch because the right of a witch or wizard to always carry their wand was one of the results of the 1692 International Confederation of Wizards. Therefore, the rules of Quidditch would imply that it is permissible for a player to use their wand on themselves or anything in the field of play that shouldn't be there such as birds or inappropriate interlopers (not mere spectators) who have illegally come onto the Pitch, as the rules strictly prohibit wand use against said spectators (Q).

58. Dementors, perhaps more than one hundred of them, although Harry can hardly be considered a reliable witness for this incident (HP3, chapter 9).

59. Dai Llewellyn was the player in question and was consumed by a Chimaera while vacationing in the Greek island of Mykonos (Q).

61. The Cleansweep One was the first mass-produced broom marketed as explicitly for sport, and therefore Quidditch, purposes. Earlier brooms such as the Moontrimmer and Silver Arrow were the choices for Quidditch of their times, but demand was far higher than supply as these remained the work of individual craftsmen (Q).

62. The Quidditch Pitch only has boundaries in two dimensions – its length (500 feet) and width (180 feet). Players and balls are only restricted by the altitude they can achieve by their own human endurance, magical laws and broom quality (Q).

63. A Bludger backbeat is a Beater technique wherein the Bludger is hit backwards. It is difficult for a Beater to get enough power to make the hit effective, and it is, of course, difficult to aim, but it's incredibly useful in

surprising the other team (Q).

64. In his mouth. In fact, from the description of him trying to get the Snitch out of his mouth, it seems possible that he may have briefly swallowed it. Certainly, Marcus Flint thought so (HP1, chapter 11).

65. Maximus Branchovich III (Q).

66. Uganda (the Patonga Proudsticks), Togo (the Tchamba Charmers), Ethiopia (the Gimbi Giant-Slayers) and Tanzania (the Sumbawanga Sunrays) (Q).

67. There is a great deal of Maori art from the 1600s depicting wizards playing Quidditch. New Zealand's Ministry of Magic has had to work quite hard, and at great cost, to make sure that this documentation of the favorite sport of wizards does not fall into Muggle hands. The art the Ministry has acquired as part of this process is on display in Wellington (Q).

68. Their name is rumored to originate from a match with the Appleby Arrows in which a Beater intentionally hit a wasps' nest at the Arrows' Seeker, retiring him from the game (Q).

69. The Vratsa Vultures (Bulgaria), the Quiberon

Quafflepunchers (France), the Heidelberg Harriers (Germany), the Bigonville Bombers (Luxembourg), Braga Broomfleet (Portugal) and the Grodzisk Goblins (Poland) (Q).

70. Stubby Boardman was the lead singer of the Hobgoblins (HP5, chapter 10).

71. Quodpot is Quidditch's rival for the affections of wizards and witches in the United States. In this game the Quaffle has been renamed a Quod and explodes. The goal is to get the ball in question into a pot at the end of the Pitch prior to said explosion (Q).

TRIVIA TIDBIT

GAMES MUGGLES PLAY

It seems likely that Quodpot is the wizarding world's stand-in for baseball. Its American popularity, along with the note that Quidditch is lately becoming increasingly popular in America (much like soccer), combined with its origins as derivative from Quidditch (much like early baseball's relationship to cricket and rounders), make this an easy conclusion even if, according to *Quidditch Through the Ages*, Japanese interest in broom sports seems limited to Quidditch.

72. Horseback Head Juggling, Head Polo and Head Hockey (HP1, chapter 8).

73. 100,000 (HP4, chapter 8).

74. It doesn't, particularly. While pieces are animated and may offer advice to the players, the rules of the game remain the same. Pieces may battle when one is moved into an occupied square, but the rules of Muggle chess apply, and which piece will win remains obvious, even if the level of brutality in the initial struggle may be a surprise (HP1, chapter 12).

75. Every five years (HP4, chapter 12).

QUEST 7

FAMOUS FAMILIES & FACES

In this Quest your knowledge of the who's who of famous witches and wizards will be tested. From Hogwarts staff members past and present, to Ministry officials, authors, Death Eaters and Order of the Phoenix members; your ability to recall names and accomplishments will be what determines your success.

Since a familiarity with *Nature's Nobility: A Wizarding Genealogy* as well as a certain number of Squibs and even Muggles may also be helpful, Muggle-borns stand just as much chance on succeeding in these quests as pure-bloods do.

In case you forgot, on this test a Dragon rating is still the best; achieving it will surely take both dedication and concentration. Phoenix follows and isn't much easier; although it will help if you've been an eager reader. Salamander, though, is a good place to begin; especially if your house isn't filled with wizarding kin.

THE QUESTIONS

1. Who is the Secret-keeper for the Order of the Phoenix?

2. What was the name of Draco's paternal grandfather?

3. When was James Potter born?

4. What do Hermione's parents do for a living?

5. What was Regulus Black's middle name?

6. Name the Weasley children from youngest to oldest.

HINTS!

Despite the problem of dates in the Harry Potter universe (discussed at length in the answer key), finding when James was born is easy if you consider this puzzle to be a bit like the riddle: "I open at the close," Harry is faced with when it comes to the Snitch Dumbledore left him. To find out when James Potter was born, find his grave.

7. Name Tom Riddle's maternal grandfather.

8. Name the siblings of Albus Dumbledore.

9. What was unique about Snape's Patronus?

10. Gilderoy Lockhart won what award from what magazine?

11. Which Weasley relative is rude to everyone?

12. Which member of the Black family was an advocate of Muggle hunting?

HiNTS!

No one ever clearly exclaims on this subject, and you'll have to compare Snape's Patronus to others you have encountered to find the answer. You'll get the most help, though, by considering the evolution of Tonks' Patronus.

13. What was Albus Dumbledore's mother's first name?

14. What happened to Neville Longbottom's parents?

15. What wood and core is Lucius Malfoy's wand made from?

16. Name the children we meet in the epilogue of Harry Potter and the Deathly Hallows.

17. Who were the members of the "gang of Slytherins" that Snape hung around with at Hogwarts?

18. When did Luna Lovegood's mother die?

HINTS!

While Lucius' wand in the books is much different than its appearance in the films, his film wand can help you solve this problem. After all, what creature could produce a heartstring long enough to fit in the walking stick wand we see Lucius use in the films?

19. Name the known pure-blood families.

20. What was the name of Bellatrix's husband's brother?

21. What happened to the middle Black sister?

22. What do Morgana, Agrippa and Ptolemy all have in common?

23. How did Remus Lupin become a werewolf?

24. In what year was Albus Dumbledore born?

HINTS!

The witch and two wizards in question 22 are all well-known, and Ron is already aware of them on his first train ride to Hogwarts. Unlike Hermione, he certainly didn't find out about them in a book, so how does he know who they are?

25. For what is Blaise Zabini's mother known?

26. Who is Inigo Imago?

27. Who is Hector Dagworth-Granger?

28. Who is the leader of the Headless Hunt?

29. Who is Ambrosius Flume?

30. Who was Arkie Alderton?

HINTS!

The name "Ambrosius" is awfully close to the word "ambrosia," the word for the food and drink of the ancient Greek gods and a colloquialism for something truly delectable. With this in mind, can you guess which store Flume owns?

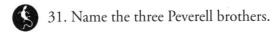

31. Name the three Peverell brothers.

32. Who was Zacharias Mumps?

33. Who was Leonard Jewkes?

34. Name the two Scrimgeours we are familiar with and the differences between them.

35. Who was Abraham Peasegood?

36. Who wrote *The Noble Sport of Warlocks*?

HINTS!

Both Scrimgeours are quite aggressive, with one being famous in sports and the other with a long and distinguished Ministry career.

37. What is the Black family motto?

38. Who was Gulliver Pokeby?

39. Who is Blenheim Stalk?

40. What is Arthur Weasley's nickname for Molly?

41. Who was Mordicus Egg?

42. Who is Ilor Dillonsby?

HINTS!

The Blacks regularly removed people from the family tree for being what they considered "blood traitors." This was one way they upheld their family motto in question. And don't forget, it's in French.

43. Barnabus the Barmy interacted with Trolls in what manner?

44. Who was Emeric Switch?

45. Who was Fingal the Fearless?

46. Who killed Emeric the Evil?

47. Who was Elliot Smethwyk?

48. Who is in charge of the Janus Thickey ward at St. Mungo's?

HiNTS!

While Emeric the Evil is first mentioned in *Harry Potter and the Sorcerer's Stone* his importance and demise doesn't become clear until *Harry Potter and the Deathly Hallows* when his relationship to the Elder Wand is discussed.

49. What was Grogan Stumps great accomplishment in terms of Ministry organization?

50. Phineas Nigellus Black was related to Sirius and Regulus Black how?

51. Who invented the Wolfsbane potion?

52. Who is the ghost of Hufflepuff?

53. Who was Alphard Black?

54. Who is Gawain Robards?

Hints!

Information about Alphard and a host of other members of the Black Family can all be found in the tour of the family tree tapestry Sirius gives Harry towards the beginning of *Harry Potter and the Order of the Phoenix.*

55. Name Nicholas Flamel's wife.

56. How would the House of Black describe itself?

57. Which member of the Black family began their habit of beheading House-elves that had outlived their usefulness?

58. What is Arabella Figg's middle name?

59. Who was Ingolfr the Iambic?

60. Who was Modesty Rabnott?

HINTS!

Although we have met Mrs. Figg prior to her appearance at a Ministry hearing, it is only when she is called to give evidence before the Wizengamot that she recites her full name for the record, thus cluing us in to her middle name.

61. Who bought Neville Longbottom his problematic toad?

62. Name Cedric Diggory's father.

63. Which books has Kennilworthy Whisp written aside from *Quidditch Through the Ages*?

64. Name Snape's father.

65. Who were Brothers Benedict and Boniface?

66. Who was Radolphus Pittiman?

HINTS!

Just like in Muggle books, it's best to look in the author's biography or other front matter of any of his available texts. Barring that, it's worth noting that all of Kennilworthy Whisp's other manuscripts were Quidditch related (there are three) and one was a biography of Dai Llewellyn.

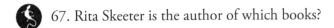

67. Rita Skeeter is the author of which books?

68. Who is Quentin Trimbell?

69. Whose retirement gave Hagrid the Care of Magical Creatures job?

70. Who was Wighelm Wigworthy?

71. Who was Dylis Derwent?

72. Who is Eldred Worple?

HĭNTS!

We never got to meet this teacher in question 69 as readers, but Dumbledore informed us, that this wizard had clearly lost at least one limb in his tenure as the Care of Magical Creatures teacher. Which either means Hagrid is less of a risk-taker than we've always suspected or you'd have to be half-mad to accept the job.

73. What is Albus Dumbledore's full name?

74. Who was a substitute teacher when Hagrid could not fulfill his Care of Magical Creatures role at Hogwarts?

75. Who ran the orphanage Tom Riddle grew up in until he went to Hogwarts?

THE ANSWERS!

 1. Dumbledore (HP5, chapter 6).

 2. Abraxas Malfoy (HP6, chapter 9).

TRIVIA TIDBIT

MAGIC, MYTH & MUGGLES

*A*braxas is a magical word, the origin of which is somewhat confused. It may or may not be related to abracadabra (discussed earlier in the entry regarding the origins of J. K. Rowling's *Avada Kedavra*). The name, which often represents some form of deity and/or the world's duality, is found in everything from Tertullian to Carl Jung and is referenced often and repeatedly in pop culture in rock songs, video games and television shows.

 3. March 27, 1960 (HP7, chapter 16).

4. They are dentists (HP1, chapter 12).

5. Arcturus (HP7, chapter 10).

6. Ginny, Ron, Fred and George, Percy, Charlie and Bill.

7. Marvolo Gaunt (HP6, chapter 10).

8. Aberforth (HP5, chapter 9) and Ariana (HP7, chapter 2).

9. Snape's Patronus, a doe, is only one of two instances (and the only confirmed one) in the entire series where someone has a Patronus of a different gender than themselves. The other instance being when Tonks' Patronus changes to something that looks suspiciously like Sirius' Animagus form but may well have been a wolf. In either case, the gender of the Patronus is not explicitly specified, however the incident follows Sirius' death and is in the midst of her pining for Lupin. So the assumption that it is male seems logical and embedded within the story. Snape's Patronus is exceptional, however, in that it seems to have always taken the form of a doe, although we

do not know at what point he learned to produce it, and there are good arguments for both early (he was clearly a gifted student) and late (he was also miserable most of the time). Based on what we see from both Tonks and Snape, this phenomenon of a cross-gender Patronus may be some sort of symptom of longing or unrequited love. A limited dataset, however, makes this difficult to determine.

10. The Most-Charming-Smile Award from *Witch Weekly*. And he didn't just win it once, but five times (HP2, chapter 6).

11. Ron's Great-Aunt Muriel (HP7, chapter 8).

12. Araminta Meliflua. Sirius says she actually tried to get the Ministry to pass a bill on the subject (HP5, chapter 7).

13. Kendra (HP7, chapter 8).

14. They were tortured by Death Eaters with the Cruciatus Curse until they became insane (HP4, chapter 30). They are now permanent residents of St. Mungo's Hospital.

15. Elm with a Dragon heartstring core (HP7, chapter 1).

TRIVIA TIDBIT

BOOK VERSUS MOVIE

In the books, Lucius Malfoy's wand is essentially like that of any other witch or wizard. However, in the films, he carries a walking stick from which the wand can be drawn, and in the film of *Harry Potter and the Order of the Phoenix* seems to use both the wand and walking stick portions in the battle at the Ministry. According to interviews with Jason Isaacs who plays the role of Lucius Malfoy in the films, the infamous snake cane was a result of his own requests.

---

16. James, Albus Severus and Lily Potter; Rose and Hugo Weasley (children of Ron and Hermione); Scorpius Malfoy; Teddy Lupin; Victoire Weasley (daughter of Bill and Fleur) (HP7, epilogue).

TRIVIA TIDBIT

MAGIC, MYTH & MUGGLES

Albus Severus doesn't just have a handful of a name, but a fascinating set of initials: ASP. Asp can refer to either a specific species of snake or be a general, although archaic, term for venomous snakes as a whole. It seems a strange name for a child that is clearly gentle and nervous in the brief look we have of him at the end of *Harry Potter and the Deathly Hallows*. This may be an allusion to Parseltongue skills that have not yet manifested. However, because the asp was also a symbol of ancient Egyptian royalty, the initials may also be a comment on the significance of both Albus Dumbledore and Severus Snape, two men who, as intellectually gifted war heroes, could both be considered as royalty in the wizarding world. Since they both held the post of headmaster of Hogwarts, it seems possible that the child named after them might one day hold the post as well.

17. Sirius alluded to this gang in chapter 25 of *Harry Potter and the Goblet of Fire*, but the only names we got were Avery and Mulciber (HP7, chapter 33) in Snape's memories of Lily.

18. When Luna was nine (HP5, chapter 38).

19. The families we can be certain of pureblood status for are the Blacks, the Gaunts, the Weasleys, the Lestranges, the Crouches, the Longbottoms and at one time possibly the Prewetts (owing to being part of the Black family by marriage). We know this either through their own bragging, observational remarks by others, or negative statements such as Sirius reporting on his mother's comments about himself and the general feelings they would have had about the Weasleys as blood-traitors (HP5, chapter 6). There are other families that may have had pureblood status that has since been relinquished or families where the name has died out but the pureblood line continues (all the Blacks may be dead, but Draco and Scorpius are still descendents of that line).

 20. Rabastan Lestrange (HP5, chapter 6).

21. Andromeda Black married Ted Tonks who was Muggle-born, and was removed from the Black family tree for it (HP5, chapter 6).

22. Morgana, Agrippa and Ptolemy all appear on Chocolate Frog cards (HP1, chapter 6).

TRIVIA TIDBIT

MAGIC, MYTH & MUGGLES

Like many of the witches and wizards appearing on the Chocolate Frog cards referenced in the Harry Potter series and later marketed as a tie-in product, Morgana, Agrippa and Ptolemy all have history, some fictional, some not, outside of the world of Harry Potter. Morgana is one of many alternate names given to the sorceress of Arthurian legend, Morgan Le Fay. Among the many famous Agrippas throughout history, the Chocolate Frog cards indicate that the Agrippa Ron refers to in *Harry Potter and the Sorcerer's Stone* is Heinrich Cornelius Agrippa, an occultist and alchemist at the beginning of the 16th century. The name Ptolemy is perhaps most famous as that of Alexander the Great's general who became king of Egypt upon Alexander's death and founded a royal line. However, the Ptolemy referred to on the Chocolate Frog card was probably the famous mathematician and astronomer who wrote several influential scientific treatises in the first half of the second century.

23. Remus Lupin was bitten by Fenrir Greyback intentionally due to a disagreement with Lupin's father (HP6, chapter 22). Greyback is repeatedly portrayed from the point we learn this information on as someone who enjoys using his status as a werewolf as a weapon, and it is for this reason he allied himself with Voldemort.

24. According to the "Wizard of the Month" feature on J. K. Rowling's website, in 1881.

25. Blaise Zabini's mother, whose first name we don't know, was apparently a "black widow" who was married seven times to wealthy men who all died mysteriously and left their fortunes to her. She was also, apparently, quite attractive (HP6, chapter 7).

26. He wrote *The Dream Oracle* (HP5, chapter 12).

27. He was the founder of The Most Extraordinary Society of Potioneers, and Slughorn, of course, wants to know if Hermione is a relative (HP6, chapter 9).

TRIVIA TIDBIT

ON MATTERS OF MATH

Calculating or even guessing the ages of characters in the Harry Potter series is an ongoing challenge for a number of reasons. First, basic information like birthdays comes from a variety of sources including the books and J. K. Rowling's website. Additionally, Rowling has had a tendency to talk about the ages of characters in vague terms that she has later contradicted (Albus Dumbledore was, in an oft-cited BBC chat, said to be "about 150," which would have made the 1881 birth date that was later released impossible). Add to this problems with calendars (The Harry Potter Lexicon: http://www.hp-lexicon.com has done impressive work on this issue that highlights just how severe and constant a problem this is), magic (Hermione lived a variety of hours and days twice due to her use of the Time Turner, possibly making her older than her birthday would indicate) and movie casting (Snape would have been 30 or 31 during Harry's first year; the actor playing him, Alan Rickman, was 54 at the time of shooting; similarly Gary Oldman, who plays Sirius Black was ten years older than the character at the time of shooting for the third film).

28. Sir Patrick Delaney-Podmore (HP2, chapter 8).

29. The owner of Honeydukes (HP6, chapter 4).

30. A broomstick designer of some fame, at least according to the man whose blood purity was being questioned in one of the Ministry sham trials under the Death Eaters (HP7, chapter 13).

31. Antioch, Cadmus and Ignotus (HP7, chapter 21).

32. He was an early chronicler of Quidditch (Q).

33. The designer of the Silver Arrow, a racing broom (Q).

34. Rufus Scrimgeour became Minister of Magic after Cornelius Fudge (HP6, chapter 1). Brutus Scrimgeour wrote *The Beater's Bible* (Q).

TRIVIA TIDBIT

MAGIC, MYTH & MUGGLES

In ancient Greek mythology Cadmus founded the city of Thebes, after being instructed to go on an unusual quest by the Oracle at Delphi that involved following a cow. Throughout his life he was in many ways a plaything of the gods; first beginning his wanderings because Zeus had stolen his sister Europa, then serving Athena and later Ares to repent for killing a serpent sacred to him. Here, several versions of the myth diverge. In one, it is said that Cadmus wishes to be a serpent if the gods are so fond of them and instantly begins to change into one. His wife later begs the gods to allow her to follow him by having her form changed as well. In either case, it is interesting that the second brother of the Beetle the Bard story, *The Tale of the Three Brothers*, who is surely Cadmus Peverell or at least a fictionalized version thereof, shares this first name and eventually dies because of his own obsession with what was lost – a girl he had once wanted to marry. This parallels nicely with the mythological Cadmus' obsession with his abducted sister and later his obsession with the slain serpent that leads to his and his wife's fantastical change.

35. The inventor of Quodpot (Q), not to be confused with Arnold Peasegood, a Ministry *Obliviator* (HP4, chapter 7).

36. Quintius Umfraville (Q).

37. Toujours Pur, which is French for "Always Pure." (HP5, chapter 6).

38. He was the author of *Why Didn't I Die When the Augery Cried?* (FB)

39. He is the author of *Muggles Who Notice* (FB).

40. Mollywobbles (HP6, chapter 5).

41. He wrote *The Philosophy of the Mundane: Why Muggles Prefer Not to Know* (FB).

42. Rita Skeeter interviewed him for her rather unflattering (but apparently, in light of revelations about the deceased Hogwarts headmaster, vaguely truthful) book about Dumbledore. He claims that he discovered eight of the twelve uses of Dragon's blood that are attributed to

Dumbledore and that Dumbledore took credit for his work (HP7, chapter 2).

43. He tried to teach Trolls ballet (HP5, chapter 18). It is unknown whether this was his only accomplishment.

44. He wrote *A Beginner's Guide to Transfiguration* (HP1, chapter 5).

45. A wizard who was legendary for reasons unknown and may have been an Aingingein champion. (Q).

46. He was killed by Egbert the Egregious (HP7, chapter 21).

47. He invented the Cushioning Charm, which is very necessary to broomstick riding (Q).

48. Miriam Strout (HP5, chapter 23).

49. Stumps structured the Ministry department concerned with magical creatures into three divisions: Beings, Beasts and Spirits (FB).

50. He was their great-great-grandfather (HP5, chapter 6).

51. It was invented by an uncle of Marcus Belby's named Damocles. Whether his surname was the same is unclear (HP6, chapter 7).

52. The Fat Friar (HP1, chapter 7).

53. He was an uncle of Sirius' who was also removed from the Black family tree, possibly because he left Sirius a significant sum of money, although it is unclear if that happened before or after Sirius' estrangement from the family (HP5, chapter 6).

54. He heads the Auror Office after Scrimgeour steps down to become Minister of Magic (HP6, chapter 15).

55. Perenelle (HP1, chapter 17).

TRIVIA TIDBIT

MAGIC, MYTH & MUGGLES

While less has been written about her than her husband both in history and fiction, Perenelle Flamel was a real woman who was married to the noted medieval alchemist, Nicholas Flamel.

---

56. "The Noble and Most Ancient House of Black" (HP5, chapter 6).

57. Elladora, who was an aunt of Sirius' (HP5, chapter 6).

58. Doreen (HP5, chapter 8).

59. A medieval poet whose works reference Quidditch (Q).

TRĬVĬA TĬDBĬT

MAGĬC, MYTH & MUGGLES

There is nothing mythological about iambs, the unit of meter whose adjectival form is Ingolfr's title. An iamb is composed of two syllables, the first one unstressed, the second one stressed. It is probably most familiar when spoken of in reference to iambic pentameter in which the bulk of Shakespeare's plays were written (many, however, contain smaller plain prose portions as well).

60. She tried to stop the first use of the Golden Snidgett in Quidditch. Despite her efforts and a hefty fine, this quickly became a tradition until the bird was replaced with today's Golden Snitch (Q).

61. His Great Uncle Algie (HP1, chapter 7).

62. Amos (HP4, chapter 9).

66. *The Wonder of the Wigtown Wanderers, He Flew Like a Madman* and *Beating the Bludgers – A Study of Defensive Strategies in Quidditch* (Q).

64. Tobias Snape (HP6, chapter 30).

65. Two Franciscan Monks who had an encounter with a Jarvey.

66. He wrote about Uric the Oddball (FB).

67. *The Life and Lies of Albus Dumbledore* (HP7, chapter 2) and *Armando Dippet: Master or Moron?* (HP7, chapter 13).

68. He wrote *The Dark Forces: A Guide to Self-Protection* (HP1, chapter 5).

69. Kettleburn (HP1, chapter 6).

70. He wrote *The Home Life and Social Habits of British Muggles* (FB).

71. She was a headmistress of Hogwarts in the 18th century and has a portrait in St. Mungo's (HP5, chapter 22).

72. He wrote *Blood Brothers: My Life Amongst the Vampires* and was a guest at The Slug Club Christmas party (HP6, chapter 15).

73. Albus Percival Wulfric Brian Dumbledore (HP5, chapter 8).

74. Wilhelmina Grubbly-Plank (HP5, chapter 11).

75. Mrs. Cole (HP6, chapter 13).

TRIVIA TIDBIT

MAGIC, MYTH & MUGGLES

Dumbledore's second name, Percival, is that of one of King Arthur's knights in Arthurian legend and is usually associated with the grail quest. This is particularly interesting in light of the revelations about Dumbledore's life in *Harry Potter and the Deathly Hallows* and his search for the vastly powerful Hallows, particularly the Resurrection Stone, which he ultimately realizes has had effects far more negative than positive on him as an individual as well as the larger wizarding world.

QUEST 8

HISTORY & LEGEND

While most aspects of the wizarding world may seem like myth or legend to the incredulous Muggle, it actually has a long and rich history complete with outlandish legends of its own.

In this Quest you will be asked to differentiate fact from fiction in the world of wizards, cite the dates of important events and show an understanding of the history that led to and included the two wars with Voldemort and the earlier war with Grindelwald.

Perhaps trickiest about this Quest is the wide range of topics covered, but it is important to remember that even in the midst of the wizarding world's most serious events things like school and Quidditch continued on.

Assuming you succeed on this Quest, a Dragon rating should cause definite delight, while success with Phoenix certainly must not be considered slight. Even Salamanders should be pleased; after all, none of these questions are anything at which to sneeze!

THE QUESTIONS

1. What Viktor Krum believes to be a Death Eater symbol on Mr. Lovegood's robe is really what?

2. What's the difference between the truth and legend of the Hallows?

3. How did The Bloody Baron die?

4. What magical creature did Luna believe Cornelius Fudge had at his command in large numbers?

5. What are the alternate names of the Elder Wand?

3. What imaginary creatures are Luna Lovegood and her father always on the hunt for?

HINTS!

When we find out the manner of the Baron's death we also find out that he continues to wear chains in penance for the reason he died.

7. Where were the Peverell brothers from?

 8. Legend says that only who can open the Chamber of Secrets?

 9. Legend says that only who can possess the Sword of Gryffindor?

 10. In the legend of the Hallows, who did the second brother use the Resurrection Stone to revive?

 11. When was the Marauder's Map created?

 12. Who was the first possessor of the Elder Wand?

HINTS!

Like Albus Dumbledore's own obsession with the Resurrection Stone the mythical brother who possessed it used it in his desire to be reunited with a woman, although the relationship between the two was different than between that of Dumbledore and his sister.

13. Harry is Hogwarts' youngest Seeker in how long?

14. When was the Whomping Willow planted at Hogwarts?

15. When was the Moontrimmer invented?

16. When was *Quidditch Through the Ages* written?

17. How much time elapsed between the opening of the Chamber of Secrets in Harry's second year and the prior opening of it?

18. When was the Snitch capture record set?

HiNTS!

Somewhat absurdly, but in typical wizarding fashion, the answer to this question cannot be found in *Quidditch Through the Ages* but rather in *Fantastic Beasts and Where to Find Them* which notes the Quidditch book for its information on the Golden Snidget.

19. When was Lily Evans born?

20. When was the Comet Trading Company founded?

21. When was the Werewolf Register created?

22. In what year did the inn at Hogsmeade serve as a headquarters of a Goblin rebellion?

23. When did Janus Thickey have his false encounter with a Leithfold?

24. When was *Hairy Snout, Human Heart* written?

HINTS!

This question is somewhat tricky because there have just been so many Goblin rebellions, but this is the only one for which we have a precise year. So if you can think of a Goblin rebellion with a date, you're thinking of the right one.

25. When did Dumbledore defeat Grindelwald?

26. When was Newt Scamander born?

27. When was the first recorded sighting of an Acromantula?

28. According to Nearly-Headless Nick, what does the Sorting Hat do other than sort?

29. What books did Hermione buy to help her understand more about wizarding history?

30. When was *Why Didn't I Die When the Augery Cry?* written?

HINTS!

Like a rather remarkable number of things in the wizarding world, the Sorting Hat seems to be a busybody, offering warnings and advice. On what subject does it pontificate?

31. What is the inscription on the Ravenclaw tiara?

32. When were Quidditch baskets replaced with goal posts?

33. When was the last time the Chudley Cannons won the League championship?

34. What is a moon frog?

35. When was the first edition of *Fantastic Beasts and Where to Find Them* published?

36. When was *Home Life and Social Habits of British Muggles* written?

HINTS!

It's been a really long time. So long, in fact, that in Ron's lifetime, the Chudley Cannons haven't even had a positive motto about their hopes for success.

37. Who had Helga Hufflepuff's cup before she was murdered by Tom Riddle?

38. Why does no one seem to know how the Bloody Baron got that way?

39. How do Dumbledore and Grindelwald meet?

40. When was the European Cup for Quidditch established?

41. When did the International Warlock Convention take place?

42. When were the Winbourne Wasps founded?

HiNTS!

It seems on some level that the center of the wizarding world is Godric's Hollow. For question 39, think of why Gellert Grindelwald is there.

43. What is written on Ariana Dumbleodre's gravestone?

44. What must you do to read the inscription on the Mirror of Erised?

45. The opal necklace that Draco eventually bought from Borgin and Burke's has claimed how many lives?

46. What is written on James and Lily Potter's gravestone?

47. Why is the Mirror of Erised dangerous?

48. Who was buried in the Godric's Hollow cemetery other than the Potters, Ignotus Peverell and Kendra and Ariana Dumbledore?

HiNTS!

Remember that we meet the opal necklace and its accompanying warning signs before Draco ever takes a direct interest in its powers. But it's in this early meeting that we find out just how deadly it is thanks to copious warnings.

49. What makes the Sorcerer's Stone such a desirable object?

50. When was the Pennifold Quaffle invented?

51. When were Gripping Charms discovered?

52. Who is the Serious Bite ward at St. Mungo's named after?

53. When was the Decree for the Reasonable Restriction of Underage Sorcery issued?

54. Who made the Sword of Gryffindor?

HINTS!

Gripping Charms were discovered in the same year the Decree for the Restriction of Underage Sorcery was issued.

55. Which former Head of Hogwarts has a portrait at St. Mungo's?

56. Who first told Tom Riddle that he was a wizard?

57. What type of wand has a reputation for being unlucky?

58. What are witches born in May likely to do?

59. If you're hoping to have a long-term effect, why shouldn't you jinx at twilight?

60. According to one of Sybil Trelawney's actual prophetic moments, how many times did Lily defy Voldemort?

HINTS!

A certain type of wand has been remarkably unlucky for a large number of people; most recently, Dumbledore, Snape and Voldemort. What type of wood is it made from?

61. How was the Elder Wand stolen from the oldest brother in *The Tale of the Three Brothers*?

62. What is the purpose of displaying the symbol of the Deathly Hallows?

63. What was Xenophilius Lovegood building on the head of Rowena Ravenclaw?

64. How does the third brother in *The Tale of the Three Brothers* become an equal with Death?

65. In what year did all 700 Quidditch fouls occur in a single match?

66. What books were Harry, Hermione and Ron unable to find Nicholas Flamel in?

HINTS!

There are several places to get this information, including in *Harry Potter and the Sorcerer's Stone* when Harry is first learning about Quidditch and in the book he learns about it from, Kennilworthy Whisp's *Quidditch Through the Ages*.

67. What did the brothers in *The Tale of the Three Brothers* do to irritate Death?

68. What did Luna Lovegood says infests mistletoe?

69. On what point does Ron disagree with Hermione about *The Tale of the Three Brothers*?

70. When did Lily and James Potter die?

71. When was the Oakshaft 79 first produced?

72. In what year did Guthrie Lochrin write on the extreme discomforts of early broom riding?

Hints!

Part of the answer can be found in the Oakshaft's name. Otherwise, it's best if you know that it wasn't first produced in Harry's lifetime, your lifetime or even Dumbledore's lifetime.

73. For how many centuries has the tapestry containing the Black Family tree been in the family?

74. When was the penalty for Stooging added to Quidditch?

75. What date is on a painting of Gunther the Violent playing Stickstock?

THE ANSWERS!

1. It is the symbol of the Deathly Hallows (HP7, chapter 8).

2. The legend of the Hallows as told in *The Tale of the Three Brothers* focuses on their having outsmarted Death to get the Hallows. While the Hallows turn out to be real, chances are the brothers Peverell just had the skill to create these magical objects themselves (HP7, chapter 21).

3. He killed himself after he killed Helena Ravenclaw (HP7, chapter 21).

4. Heliopaths, which Luna said are fire spirits (HP5, chapter 17).

5. "The Deathstick" and "The Wand of Destiny" (HP7, chapter 21).

6. The Crumple-Horned Snorkack (HP5, chapter 13).

7. Godric's Hollow (HP7, chapter 16).

8. The Heir of Slytherin (HP2, chapter 9).

9. Only a true Gryffindor. Since the sword is used at various times by Dumbledore, Neville, Ron and Harry, this doesn't seem to have as much to do with ancestry as it does with upholding Gryffindor principles. On the other hand, as all of them are connected to old-wizarding families, it is possible that they could all be distant relations (HP2, chapter 18 provides the first mention of who can use the sword).

10. A woman he had desired to marry (HP7, chapter 21).

11. In the Marauders' fifth year (HP3, chapter 18).

12. Antioch Peverell (HP7, chapter 21).

13. A century (HP1, chapter 9).

14. During or immediately prior to Remus Lupin's arrival at Hogwarts. It was put there specifically to protect the Shrieking Shack and Remus' secret (HP3, chapter 18).

15. 1901 (Q).

TRÍVÍA TÍDBÍT

GAMES MUGGLES PLAY

Muggles also had a momentous year in sports and transportation in 1901 with a huge reshuffling of the American baseball leagues and New York State becoming the first U.S. state to require license plates for cars. The longest covered bridge in the world at that time also opened in town of Hartland, New Brunswick in Canada.

16. 1952 (FB). This date, however, is particularly confusing and may refer to an early edition of the book. The copy of *Quidditch Through the Ages* that we as Muggles have access to clearly references several major dates in the history of Quidditch well after the 1952 publishing date cited in *Fantastic Beasts and Where to Find Them*, meaning there is either an error in Newt Scamander's dating or *Quidditch Through the Ages* has received some recent updates.

 17. Approximately fifty years earlier (HP2, chapter 15).

18. In 1921 Roderick Plumpton caught the Golden Snitch in three and a half seconds (Q).

19. January 30, 1960 (HP7, chapter 16).

20. 1929 (Q).

Trivia Tidbit

Magic, Muggles & History

While the Comet Trading Company was being founded, American Muggles were reeling from the crash of the New York Stock Exchange, which ushered in the Great Depression. Before the economic disaster, though, 1929 also saw the founding of the Academy Awards and the Graf Zeppelin launch a flight around the world. The trip took over 21 days, which must have seemed ridiculous by wizarding standards.

21. 1947 (FB).

22. 1612 (HP3, chapter 5).

23. 1973 (FB).

24. 1975 (FB).

Trivia Tidbit

Magic, Muggles & Science

At the end of 1612, Galileo observed Neptune for the first time, but did not recognize it as a planet and assumed it to be a star. Perhaps he should have consulted the Centaurs.

---

25. 1945 (HP1, chapter 6).

26. 1897 (FB).

27. 1794 (FB).

28. It gives a warning when Hogwarts is in great danger (HP5, chapter 11).

29. *Modern Magical History, The Rise and Fall of the Dark Arts* and *Great Wizarding Events of the Twentieth Century* (HP1, chapter 6).

30. 1824 (FB).

31. "Wit beyond measure is man's greatest treasure" (HP7, chapter 29).

32. 1883 (Q).

33. 1892 (Q).

TRIVIA TIDBIT

GAMES MUGGLES PLAY

While the Chudley Cannons were enjoying their last taste of victory for a very long time to come, American Muggles saw the birth of basketball in Massachusetts. Meanwhile in England, the Football League took over the Football Alliance and split into two divisions.

---

34. Moon frogs, are, predictably, frogs found on the moon. But since our only knowledge of them comes from a Quibbler article, which interviews someone who claims to have gotten to the moon on a Cleansweep 6 (of all things!), there's a good chance that these are merely

creatures of legend (HP5, chapter 11).

 35. 1927, although the book was first commissioned in 1918 (FB).

36. 1987 (FB).

TRIVIA TIDBIT

MAGICAL MOMENTS

It may seem alarming to see a citation for a book on Muggles in a text called *Fantastic Beasts and Where to Find Them*. However, be assured that this reference is in regards to helping readers find a source for understanding more about Muggle electricity, not any sort of classification of Muggles as Beasts.

---

37. Hepzibah Smith (HP6, chapter 20).

 38. Most people are scared of him and when Sir Nicholas is asked about it, he notes that he thought it would be rude to inquire (HP1, chapter 7).

39. Grindelwald had a great aunt in Godric's Hollow, whom he visited after being expelled from Durmstrang. It is there that he met Albus Dumbledore (HP7, chapter 18).

40. 1652 (Q).

41. 1289 (HP2, chapter (9).

42. 1312 (Q).

43. "Where your treasure is, there will your heart be also" (HP7, chapter 16).

44. The inscription is written backwards, in mirror writing. However, the letters are not broken up into words correctly, making the inscription seem more like a foreign language (HP1, chapter 12).

45. Nineteen, all Muggle (HP2, chapter 4).

46. In addition to their birth and death dates it says "The last enemy that shall be destroyed is death" (HP7, chapter 16).

TRIVIA TIDBIT

MAGICAL MOMENTS

Harry is initially alarmed by the inscription on the grave of his parents, stating that it strikes him as a Death Eater sentiment. It is Hermione that has to explain to him that this defeat of death is about living in memory or perhaps spirit, not related to Voldemort's ugly quest for immortality.

47. Because it shows what the viewer desires most of all, it is easy to become addicted to it. Dumbledore says that men have starved in front of it or been driven mad by the things it shows (HP1, chapter 12).

48. A member of the Abbott family, possibly related to Hannah, whose first name is not noted (HP7, chapter 16).

49. The Sorcerer's Stone produces the Elixir of Life, which when taken regularly can essentially provide immortality. It can also provide unlimited wealth. Finally, there is only one known Stone in the world (HP1, chapter 17).

50. Shortly after or perhaps during 1711 (Q).

TRIVIA TIDBIT

MAGIC & MUGGLES

While wizards got the Pennifold Quaffle, Muggles got the tuning fork, which was invented by John Shore in 1711.

 51. 1875 (Q).

TRIVIA TIDBIT

MAGIC, MUGGLES & HISTORY

The year 1875 wasn't just a busy year in the wizarding world, but a busy year in the Muggle world as well. Kwang-su became the emperor of China, Carmen received its first performance in Paris and the notoriously corrupt New York politician, Boss Tweed, escaped prison, fleeing to Cuba and then Spain.

52. Dai Llewellyn (HP5, chapter 21).

53. 1875 (HP2, chapter 2).

54. Ragnuk the First (HP7, chapter 25).

55. Dilys Derwent (HP5, chapter 22).

56. Albus Dumbledore (HP6, chapter 13).

57. Elder. This is also a superstition of the wizarding world and Ron wondered if it could be related to the Elder Wand itself (HP7, chapter 21).

58. According to a superstition Ron cited as the type of thing his mother knew, marry a Muggle (HP7, chapter 21).

59. Jinx. According to Ron Weasley there is a common wizarding superstition that a jinx cast twilight will be "undone by midnight" (HP7, chapter 21).

60. Three times (HP5, chapter 37).

61. After killing an enemy with it he went to a pub and bragged about the wand he had taken from Death. That night a wizard stole the wand and murdered him while he was sleeping off his wine (HP7, chapter 21).

62. Those who believe in the existence of the Hallows wear the sign to alert others that they are searching for them (as Xenophilius Lovegood says all believers are) in hopes that they might receive some help on their quest for the objects (HP7, chapter 21).

63. It is a device designed, it seems based on Xenophilius Lovegood's description of the components, to help the wearer accept the extraordinary, be free from distraction and have heightened thought processes (HP7, chapter 20).

64. He hides under the Invisibility Cloak to avoid Death most of his life, but finally takes it off as an old man when he is ready to die. Thus Death comes for him and they respond to each other as friends and equals (HP7, chapter 21).

65. 1473 (HP1, chapter 11).

TRIVIA TIDBIT

MAGIC & MUGGLES

While chaos reigned on the Quidditch Pitch, great astronomer and mathematician, Copernicus, was born in Poland. He posited today's scientific given, that the earth moves around the sun, and was also involved in monetary reform.

66. *Great Wizards of the Twentieth Century, Notable Magical Names of Our Time, Important Modern Magical Discoveries,* and *A Study of Recent Developments in Wizardry* (HP1, chapter 12).

67. They used their wands to cross a dangerous river that should have killed them (HP7, chapter 21).

68. Nargles (HP5, chapter 21).

69. Ron said that his mother told *The Tale of the Three Brothers* such that the initial encounter with Death happened at midnight, as opposed to the twilight of Hermione's version (HP7, chapter 21).

70. October 31, 1981. This piece of information comes to us throughout the series since we are repeatedly told that Harry's parents died on Halloween when the boy was one year old. We get the date most clearly and unarguably, however, from their tombstone in chapter sixteen of *Harry Potter and the Deathly Hallows*.

71. 1879 (Q).

TRIVIA TIDBIT

MAGIC & MUGGLES

It is possible that the production of the Oakshaft 79 may be the least interesting thing that happened in 1879, at least if you're a Muggle and you've never heard of a flying broom before. English writer E.M. Forster, physicist Albert Einstein, actress Ethel Barrymore, poet Wallace Stevens and revolutionary Leon Trotsky were all born in 1879. Surely, the stars must have been aligned quite uniquely that year.

 72. 1107 (Q).

73. Seven (HP5, chapter 6).

74. 1884 (Q).

75. 1105 (Q).

QUEST 9

THE WIZARDING WARS

The wizard wars are perhaps most central to the story of Harry Potter. While at the beginning of the series Harry's struggle against Voldemort may have seemed personal, by its end it was clear that Harry had become merely the latest central figure in a set of issues and conflicts that have been plaguing the wizarding world for decades if not centuries.

This Quest focuses on the three wizarding wars for which we have detailed information: Dumbledore's struggle with Grindelwald, the first war with Voldemort that ended with the death of Harry's parents and Harry's own survival of the killing curse and the second war with Voldemort that concludes the series. Know war heroes and villains, casualties, tactics, chronology and events. Keep track of crosses and double crosses, understand the complex magic governing wand ownership and attempt to distinguish personal motivations from larger causes.

A Salamander rating means you're clever enough to keep yourself safe. Phoenix will show you care about the wizarding world's fate, while success with Dragon implies you're brave, daring and simply great!

THE QUESTIONS

1. Why did Remus regret marrying Tonks?

2. Why wasn't Voldemort able to kill Harry at Godric's Hollow?

3. Why was Bathilda Bagshot unwilling to speak in front of Hermione?

4. Why was Hedwig mad at Harry at the time of her death?

5. Name the seven Horcruxes.

6. Name the members of the original Order of the Phoenix.

HINTS!

Remember that Bathilda Bagshot is not what she seems at the start of her encounter with Harry and Hermione.

7. Who did Voldemort torture at Malfoy Mansion?

8. Where did Bertha Jorkins disappear?

9. Name the fates of each Weasley by the end of the second war with Voldemort.

10. Where was the Lost Diadem finally found?

11. Why was Kreacher able to escape the cave after drinking the poison protecting the Horcrux that Regulus Black eventually stole?

12. Describe the chain of ownership of the Elder Wand as related to Dumbledore's death.

HINTS!

Weasleys seem to suffer only one major event, so once you've recalled a serious war wound to a Weasley, chances are nothing else happens to them. When answering this question don't forget to include the often absent Percy, as well as parents Arthur and Molly.

13. What argument did the Ministry under the Death Eaters use to justify Muggle-born persecution?

14. What is the motto of Nuremgard?

15. Who were the faculty at Hogwarts under Snape?

16. What skill was Snape said to have learned "from his master" in *Harry Potter and the Deathly Hallows*?

17. Name the known female Death Eaters.

18. Why did Dumbledore trust Snape?

HINTS!

Other than Snape himself, there are only two significant faculty changes we know about during his brief tenure as headmaster.

19. What did Ron do to Draco during the Battle of Hogwarts?

20. Describe the memorial at Godric's Hollow.

21. What clothes is Dobby buried with?

22. How did Hermione keep her parents safe?

23. Who impersonated Harry in order to keep him safe during his final flight from the Dursleys?

24. Where did Harry, Ron and Hermione run into Dean Thomas?

HINTS!

There are three Weasleys, one soon-to-be Weasley and one later-to-be-Weasley among the six Harry impersonators.

25. What Weasley Wizard Wheezes' products were employed in the war effort?

26. Voldemort used Fenrir Greyback to what purposes in the wars?

27. What caused Herbert Chorley's hospitalization?

28. Name the members of the Bones family killed by Death Eaters.

29. What were the Snatchers?

30. Who were the Peverell brothers?

HiNTS!

Just a reminder, Herbert Chorley was a Muggle, and while it's true, saying he was attacked by Death Eaters is not enough to answer this question.

31. What role did Horace Slughorn play in Tom Riddle's plan for immortality?

32. What was Ron able to do with the Deluminator other than manage light?

33. What was Harry labeled as by the Death Eater-controlled Ministry?

34. Ollivander told Voldemort that who had the Elder Wand?

35. Why did Voldemort break into Dumbledore's tomb?

36. Who did Hermione Polyjuice herself into in order to break into Gringotts?

HiNTS!

For the answer to this question, you can check Arthur Weasley's file in the Death Eater-controlled Ministry.

37. What is Aberforth Dumbelore's Patronus?

38. What was the only secret route into or out of Hogwarts during Snape's administration?

39. Who were River, Royal, Romulus and Rapier?

40. What was the graffiti Neville and the DA put up on the castle?

41. What was the name of the rebel's broadcast on the WNN?

42. Which two Hogwarts classes changed under the Carrows and how?

HINTS!

These are code names and characters you've met before. Royal and Romulus' code names most hint at their real ones.

43. How does one get into the Ravenclaw common room?

44. Who is the Grey Lady?

45. What spells did Hermione use to protect the campsites that she, Ron and Harry used?

46. Voldemort intended to do away with the Hogwarts Sorting ceremony and unite all the students under one banner. Which banner was that?

47. Who killed Bellatrix Lestrange?

48. Who did Hermione claim to be when captured by Greyback and Scabior?

HINTS!

Among the spells Hermione used to keep the campsite safe were those that muffle any sound they might be making as well as those that repel Muggles.

49. Despite the destruction at Godric's Hollow, why did the Invisibility Cloak survive for Harry to inherit?

50. What were the steps necessary for tuning into PotterWatch?

51. Name all the obstacles that were guarding the Sorcerer's Stone.

52. According to Quirrell, Voldemort said there was no good or evil, only what?

53. What were the two known passwords for PotterWatch?

54. Which potion did Harry have to drink to move forward through the obstacles protecting the Sorcerer's Stone?

HINTS!

This question takes you back to the second war with Voldemort before everyone knew it was a war. Remember that several different Hogwarts' professors designed or selected the obstacles protecting the Stone and each obstacle reflects their own specialties and interests.

55. As a student, who did Tom Riddle frame as the Heir of Slytherin?

56. For what offense did Harry receive his "I must not tell lies" punishment?

57. Name the residents of Spinner's End immediately before the start of the second War with Voldemort.

58. Why was Harry required to spend time at the Dursleys'?

59. Who bound the Unbreakable Vow between Narcissa Malfoy and Severus Snape?

60. What ingredients did Voldemort need in the graveyard at Little Hangleton to restore himself to proper physical form?

Hints!

Remember that Snape was not living alone, nor did he seem to be particularly enjoying his roommate situation. After all, would you really want a rat in your house?

61. How did Severus Snape and Lily Evans first meet?

62. For what reason did Draco become less fond of Snape?

63. Who did the Death Eaters go after to try to stop Neville Longbottom's resistance?

64. Why did Snape accuse Dumbledore of using him?

65. How did the Order of the Phoenix get the idea to use Potter-decoys in Harry's final exit from the Dursley home?

66. Why was the Chamber of Secrets opened during the Battle of Hogwarts?

Hints!

Since Neville's parents have been in St. Mungo's since the end of the first war with Voldemort, the Death Eaters had to go after a different relative this time.

67. Who returned Harry's "body" to Hogwarts?

68. Why did Death Eaters torture Michael Corner?

69. Describe the chain of ownership of the Horcrux Regulus Black stole.

70. Name the casualties of Harry's escape from the Dursleys.

71. Where did Ron go when he left Harry and Hermione?

72. Who gave the sword of Gryffindor to Harry in *Harry Potter and the Deathly Hallows*?

HINTS!

Remember that Harry wasn't just handed this sword. Rather he was led to it by something whose identity he wasn't clear of at the time.

73. Who should Voldemort have killed instead of Snape?

74. Why was Draco Malfoy ordered to kill Dumbledore?

75. Describe Harry's multiple connections to Voldemort.

THE ANSWERS !

1. Lupin felt that he turned Tonks into an outcast by marrying her and stated that her own parents were revolted. He was also concerned about what lycanthropic tendencies he might have passed on to their unborn child. Additionally, it can be argued that he implied he was pressured into the marriage (HP7, chapter 11).

2. Lily, by sacrificing her life for Harry, unknowingly placed an enchantment on him that protected him from Voldemort's killing curse at Godric's Hollow. Versions of this fact are repeated throughout the series, but the most authoritative announcement of it probably comes from Harry's conversation with a posthumous Dumbledore in chapter 35 of *Harry Potter and the Deathly Hallows*.

3. Bathilda Bagshot, who was really Nagini hiding inside her corpse, did not want to speak in front of Hermione as the fact that she was using Parseltongue would have been readily apparent to Hermione, who cannot speak or understand the language (HP7, chapter 17).

4. She was angry with Harry over how much time she had to spend in her cage (HP7, chapter 2).

5. Tom Riddle's diary (HP2), Marvolo Gaunt's ring (HP6), Salazar Slytherin's locket (HP6), Helga Hufflepuff's cup (HP6), Rowena Ravenclaw's diadem (HP7), Nagini (HP7), and Harry Potter (HP7). Many of these artifacts were initially introduced before we or Harry were aware of the Horcrux issue, and Harry was, of course, only partially a Horcrux thanks to the part of Voldemort's soul that fragmented and became lodged in him when *Avada Kedavra* failed to kill him as a baby (HP7, chapter 35).

6. Mad-Eye Moody, Albus Dumbledore, Dedalus Diggle, Marlene McKinnon, Frank Longbottom, Alice Longbottom, Emmeline Vance, Remus Lupin, Benjy Fenwick, Edgar Bones, Sturgis Podmore, Caradoc Dearborn, Rubeus Hagrid, Elphias Dodge, Gideon Prewett, Aberforth Dumbledore, Dorcas Meadowes, Sirius Black, James Potter, Lily Potter and Peter Pettigrew. The listing of the individuals in the photo makes it unclear whether Gideon Prewett's brother, Fabian, was also a member (HP5, chapter 9).

7. Charity Burbage (HP1, chapter 7), who was probably not the first, nor the last to meet such a fate at Malfoy Manor.

8. Albania (HP4, chapter 1).

9. Ginny is unscathed and marries Harry at some point after the end of the war (HP7, epilogue). Ron is unscathed and has finally gotten together with Hermione (HP7, chapter 31) whom he also later marries (HP7, epilogue). George lost an ear (HP7, chapter 5). Fred died (HP7, chapter 31), Percy is unscathed and reunited with the family (HP7, chapter 30). Charlie is unscathed. Bill has been bitten by Greyback while Greyback was in human form, giving him some lycanthropic tendencies (HP6, chapter 27) and marries Fleur (HP7, chapter 8). Molly kills Bellatrix (HP7, chapter 36) and is physically unharmed. Arthur Weasley also survives without additional injury after his encounter with Nagini in HP5.

10. In the Room of Requirement in its function as the place where all things are hidden (HP7, chapter 31).

11. He Disapparated (HP7, chapter 10).

TRÍVÍA TÍDBÍT

MAGÍCAL MOMENTS

K reacher's survival after drinking the poison that guarded the locket Horcrux is one of the weirdest and most ambiguous things in the Harry Potter series. The easy argument, of course, is that as a House-elf the poison affected him differently than it would a mortal human. The next logical argument may be that the water he drank from the lake filled with Inferi somehow acted as an antidote, although that's hardly a solution to the problem of escape from the cave when the House-elf himself noted that the Inferi dragged him under for a time. Under continued questioning about his escape, all Kreacher was able to say was that Regulus told him to come back. This led Ron to deduce that Kreacher Disapparated, which Harry said was not possible from the cave in question. Ron explained this by saying that House-elf magic is different, which seems to be consistent with what we know from House-elves Apparating and Disapparating within Hogwarts. All this logic, though, doesn't change the fact that ultimately Kreacher didn't die and was able to escape the cave simply because his beloved master ordered him to return. This effectively highlights just how creepy the nature of House-elf slavery in the wizarding world is.

12. When Dumbledore died, he was the owner of the Elder Wand. Voldemort believed that Snape, having killed Dumbledore, was the new master of it. However, because Snape's killing of Dumbledore had been an agreed upon plan between the two men that Dumbledore had actually requested, Snape was not the master of the Elder wand. Rather, Draco Malfoy, who had disarmed Dumbledore and whose orders from Voldemort to kill the headmaster had led to Snape's Unbreakable Vow and the necessity of his killing Dumbledore, was at that moment the master of the wand. Harry had taken Draco's wand from him prior to the final battle at Hogwarts. Therefore, Harry was the true master of the Elder wand at the time of his final battle with Voldemort, despite the fact that he never technically laid hands on it (HP7, chapter 36).

13. The Department of Mysteries in the Death Eater-controlled Ministry issued the results of a study that claimed magic can only be passed down from wizards and witches to their children. As such, the Ministry then claimed that where there is no wizarding ancestry, the magical skills in question had probably been taken by force (HP7, chapter 11).

 14. "For the Greater Good" (HP7, chapter 8).

15. The faculty were largely the same as in Harry's sixth year, with Snape having replaced Dumbledore as headmaster, with Alecto Carrow having taken over Muggle Studies and Amycus Carrow having taken over what was Defense Against the Dark Arts (and becomes just the Dark Arts) (HP7, chapter 27).

16. An ability to fly or at least soar long distances, such that his leap from a Hogwarts window did him no discernable harm (HP7, chapter 30).

17. Bellatrix Black and Alecto Carrow. Narcissa Black, while clearly a Voldemort sympathizer, is not known to be Marked and ultimately betrays him (HP7, chapter 36).

18. Dumbledore trusted Snape because he pledged "anything" to Dumbledore if he would only keep Lily and her family safe. That failed, because Pettigrew was their Secret-keeper, but Snape vowed at Dumbledore's prodding to help protect Harry. As seen in "The Prince's Tale" throughout his difficult friendship with Dumbledore, Severus repeatedly revealed his continued dedication to

the cause and his enduring love for Lily (HP7, chapter 33).

19. Ron punched Draco in the face after he and Harry saved him for the second time (HP7, chapter 32).

20. James and Lily's house was left with the damage caused the night they died and a small plaque was added to inform visitors that it was there as a memorial. Graffiti, including names and well wishes left over the time since the attack, covered the sign (HP7, chapter 17).

21. Harry's jacket, Ron's socks, Dean's wool hat (HP7, chapter 24).

22. She changed their memories so that they believed themselves to be Wendell and Monica Wilkins who wanted to move to Australia. The spell also made sure that they did not know they had a daughter (HP7, chapter 6).

TRIVIA TIDBIT

MAGICAL MOMENTS

Hermione told Ron and Harry that she would find her parents and lift the spell after the war if she survived. However, no mention of the resolution of this is made in the epilogue. While we have known since the first book that Harry could have as easily gone to Slytherin as Gryffindor, this incident, which shows us a ruthless and cunning Hermione, makes us think that the same could well have been true of her.

23. Ron, Hermione, Fred, George, Fleur and Mundungus (HP7, chapter 4).

24. They found Dean amongst the prisoners once they were captured by Greyback and the Snatchers he seemed to be working with (HP7, chapter 23).

25. Extendable Ears; Shield Gloves, Hats and Cloaks; Instant Darkness Powder; Decoy Detonators (HP6, chapter 6).

26. In order to gain the support of reluctant witches

and wizards, Voldemort threatened many of them with the possibility of Greyback changing their children into Werewolves (HP6, chapter 16).

27. A weird side effect from the Imperius curse that caused him to quack like a duck. He was also repeatedly violent towards St. Mungo's healers (HP6, chapter 1).

28. Edgar Bones (HP5, chapter 1), Amelia Bones (HP6, chapter 1) and a Mrs. Bones (HP1, chapter 4) whose relationship to the rest of the family is unclear.

29. The Snatchers were people trying to earn money from Ministry rewards by rounding up Muggle-borns and those classified as blood traitors (HP7, chapter 19).

30. The Peverell Brothers were three brothers who were the original owners and perhaps creators of the Deathly Hallows (HP7, chapter 21).

31. It was he that told Tom Riddle about Horcruxes (HP6, chapter 27).

32. Ron used it to return to Harry and Hermione (HP7, chapter 19).

TRIVIA TIDBIT

MAGICAL MOMENTS

Ron's use of the Deluminator to find Harry and Hermione is fascinating. Instead of the device merely acting as a Portkey, it generated a sphere of magic that Ron described as looking similar to a Portkey. This then entered Ron, and he said he felt that he knew where he needed to go and was able to Apparate to where Harry was by the lake. This is one of several examples throughout *Harry Potter and the Deathly Hallows* of people learning to trust themselves and their own abilities in order to help a larger cause.

33. Undesirable No. 1 (HP7, chapter 13).

34. Gregorovitch (HP7, chapter 24).

35. To retrieve the Elder Wand that he believed himself able to master once he had killed Snape (HP7, chapter 24). Whether Voldemort had decided to kill Snape at that point is unclear.

36. Bellatrix Lestrange (HP7, chapter 26).

37. A goat (HP7, chapter 28).

38. The tunnel leading from the Room of Requirement as it exists under the control of Dumbledore's Army to the portrait of Ariana Dumbledore in the Hog's Head Inn (HP7, chapter 28).

TRIVIA TIDBIT

MAGICAL MOMENTS

The usual "secret" passages into and out of Hogwarts that appeared on the Marauder's Map and were known to the Weasley twins and probably other students over the years were, according to Neville Longbottom, sealed up before the start of the year under Snape's school leadership (HP7, chapter 29).

39. Lee Jordan, Kingsley Shacklebolt, Remus Lupin and Fred Weasley, who was known as "Rodent" until he protested (HP7, chapter 22).

40. "Dumbledore's Army, Still Recruiting" was the example Neville sited, although it seems clear that was just one of many (HP7, chapter 29).

41. PotterWatch (HP7, chapter 22).

TRIVIA TIDBIT

MAGIC, MACHINES & MUGGLES

While supporters of the Order of the Phoenix may have been tuning into PotterWatch during the second war with Voldemort, Muggle fans of Harry Potter have been tuning into a number of podcasts for years now. These range from general interest shows on the overall Harry Potter phenomenon such as The Leaky Cauldron's Pottercast, MuggleNet's Mugglecast or the latest major entry to the field, SpinnerCast, to more specifically focused shows such as the all-Snape-all-the-time SnapeCast.

42. Muggle Studies became compulsory and focused on how Muggles were like animals. Defense Against the

Dark Arts morphed into merely a tutorial in the Dark Arts in which students practiced the Cruciatus Curse on those who had been given detention (HP7, chapter 29).

43. By correctly answering a question (HP7, chapter 30).

44. The Grey Lady is Helena Ravenclaw, the daughter of Rowena (HP7, chapter 31).

45. Salvio Hexia, Protego Totalum, Repello Muggletum, Muffliato and Cave Inimicum (HP7, chapter 14).

46. Slytherin (HP7, chapter 36).

47. Molly Weasley (HP7, chapter 36).

48. Penelope Clearwater (HP7, chapter 23).

49. Dumbledore had, according to Sirius' account of what Lily said, borrowed the Invisibility Cloak. Harry deduced that Dumbledore had wanted to examine it to see if it was one of the Hallows. When the Potters died while the cloak was in Dumbledore's possession he wound up holding onto it, both out of his own interest and in turn to keep it safe for Harry. It is unclear if it would have survived or, if it had, if it would have passed to Harry had

it not been in Dumbledore's possession that night (HP7, chapter 22).

50. One had to tune to the right station and say the right password (HP7, chapter 20).

51. Fluffy, Devil's Snare, the winged keys, the giant chessboard, the logic puzzle and the Mirror of Erised (HP1, chapter 16).

52. "Only power" (HP1, chapter 17).

53. "Albus" and "Mad-Eye" (HP7, chapter 22).

54. The potion in the smallest bottle of the seven (HP1, chapter 16).

55. Hagrid (HP2, chapter 15).

56. Saying that Voldemort had returned. Umbridge claimed this was a lie and that Harry was just saying it to get attention (HP5, chapter 13).

57. Severus Snape and Peter Pettigrew, who was now seemingly exclusively, called Wormtail (HP6, chapter 1).

58. There was a Protective Charm that kept Harry safe as long as he was under sevemteen and returned to the Dursley house each year. The spell, enabling and requiring Harry to leave the Dursley home for the last time, concluded when Harry and the Dursleys all fled to safety at more or less the same time, rendering the house no more a home (HP7, chapter 3).

59. Bellatrix Lestrange (HP6, chapter 1).

60. Bone from Tom Riddle Sr.'s grave ("bone of the father"), Wormtail's hand ("flesh from a servant") and Harry's blood ("blood of the enemy") (HP4, chapter 32).

61. Snape and Lily grew up in the same town, and they first encountered each other when Snape, who had been spying on her at a playground, informed her that she was a witch (HP7, chapter 33).

62. During "The Prince's Tale" we saw Snape correct Dumbledore's assertion that Draco was fond of the professor. The spy noted that this was less true now that he had risen high enough within Death Eater ranks that Draco felt Snape had pushed his father out of a position of favor (HP7, chapter 33).

63. Just as the Death Eaters threatened the children of many witches and wizards to get their support, they then attempted to quell dissent within Hogwarts by going after the families of students. In Neville's case they attacked his grandmother. But she escaped, putting Dawlish in St. Mungo's in the process (HP7, chapter 29).

64. Again, this comes from one of their discussions as seen during "The Prince's Tale." Snape was aghast that he had agreed to help Dumbledore in order to protect Lily's son only to find out that Dumbledore had been preparing Harry to die to defeat Voldemort. Snape was also outraged that Dumbledore expected him to be the one to hasten his death in order to protect Draco's soul while displaying seemingly little concern for the state of his own (HP7, chapter 33).

65. The idea came from Dumbledore himself. He told it to Snape who he then instructed to give the idea to Mundungus Fletcher via a Confundus Charm (HP7, chapter 33).

66. Ron and Hermione opened the Chamber to get Basilisk fangs to use to destroy the remaining Horcruxes. Opening the Chamber still required the use of Parseltongue, but Ron was able to imitate Harry's use of the language (HP7, chapter 31).

67. Hagrid (HP7, chapter 36).

68. He released a first-year student the Carrows had chained up. The Carrows tortured him severely enough that, according to Neville, at least some overt dissent was quelled (HP7, chapter 29).

69. Salazar Slytherin's locket was first taken from the Gaunt's by Tom Riddle, who, once he had turned it into a Horcrux, placed it in the cave. From there, it was stolen by Regulus Black who died to get it and gave it to Kreacher to bring back to Grimauld Place to destroy (HP7, chapter 10). Kreacher was unable to do this, and the locket was eventually stolen by Mundungus Fletcher who then sold it to Umbridge (HP7, chapter 11). It was to get the locket from Umbridge that Harry, Ron and Hermione broke into the Ministry of Magic. After they had retrieved it, the three of the them took turns wearing it, until finally destroying it by stabbing it with the Sword of Gryffindor (HP7, chapter 19).

70. Hedwig, George's ear and Mad-Eye Moody (HP7, chapter 5).

71. Unfortunately for Ron he Disapparated into a group of Snatchers. After escaping them by claiming to be Stan Shunpike, he attempted to rejoin Harry and Hermione, but they had left that camping location by the

time Ron was able to get to it. It seems he then went back to the Burrow until he heard Hermione's voice from the Deluminator and was able to use it to get back to her and Harry (HP7, chapter 19).

72. Snape's Patronus, unknown to Harry as such at that time, led Harry to the Sword of Gryffindor frozen in a small lake (HP7, chapter 19).

TRIVIA TIDBIT

MAGICAL MOMENTS

Amidst the beauty of the scene in which Harry is led to the sword of Gryffindor lying frozen in the water, is an interesting and potentially strange allusion to Arthurian myth. The Lady of the Lake in Arthurian legend has actually represented many different characters as the story has evolved through the centuries. However, in many versions of the tale, it is this figure who gives Arthur Excalibur, the sword he needs to reach his destiny. In others, she is also said to be an apprentice to Merlin, who, after learning his secrets and rejecting his advances, betrays him, trapping him under the lake. All of this makes an interesting, if somewhat messy, parallel with Snape's Patronus leading Harry to the sword and the former professor's conflicted relationships with Voldemort, Dumbledore and even Lily.

73. By the time of the final battle, Voldemort would have needed to kill Harry to gain control of the Elder Wand. To have had control of the wand before his duel with Harry he would have needed to defeat Draco several weeks earlier (HP7, chapter 36).

74. Aside from Voldemort's desire to have Dumbledore out of the way, it was assumed that Draco would fail. According to Snape, giving Draco the task was merely a way for Voldemort to punish Lucius (HP7, chapter 33).

75. Harry has two main connections to Voldemort. The first relates to their matched wand cores, something that is a factor in Voldemort's desire for the Elder Wand. The other is that Harry accidentally contains a part of Voldemort's soul. On the night that Voldemort killed Harry's parents his soul was so unstable that when the Killing Curse failed to eliminate Harry, a part of Voldemort fractured and became part of Harry – hence their periodic telepathic connection and Harry's ability to speak Parseltongue (HP7, chapter 35).

TRIVIA TIDBIT

MAGIC, MYTH & MUGGLES

Harry's connection to Voldemort is, throughout the series, a frequent cause of stabbing headaches for "The Boy Who Lived." So much so that Fred Sheftell, a doctor at the New England Center for Headache and his colleagues diagnosed Harry as a "probable" migraine sufferer as a way to highlight the problem of migraines and other headache conditions in young adults. The full details of the diagnosis appear in the American Headache Society's journal.